BLACK AND SEXY

This book offers a unique understanding of African American populations and their articulation of sexuality and race by introducing a comprehensive sexological model, Black Sexual Epistemology.

Tracie Q. Gilbert draws from theoretical perspectives of anti-Blackness, ethno-sexuality, Performative Blackness and African-centered epistemology to implicate race as an inextricable factor in the sexual structures and schema of African American people. Chapters identify and introduce a sex-positive and comprehensive sexological model, Black Sexual Epistemology, through which Black sexuality can be understood and navigated in the contemporary era. This model presents empirical data for effectively applying previous critical race perspectives and uniquely demonstrates how Black sexual experience can be better understood and reimagined for greater community development and healing.

This book is essential reading for practicing sex therapists, marriage and family therapists and clinical social workers working with these populations as well as for academics and students of sexology, sex education, sex therapy, social work, marriage and family therapy, public health, Black/African American studies and LGBTQ studies. It will also be of interest to general audiences who appreciate culturally centered sexological scholarship.

Tracie Q. Gilbert is an educator, researcher and consultant who pursues sexual healing for Black people and racial justice in sex ed spaces. She is the owner of Thembi Anaiya LLC and an assistant professor at Widener University's Center for Human Sexuality Studies.

"What's compelling about Dr. Gilbert's book is that she invites us to think critically about the convergence of sexuality and race and frames the two elusive constructs in a manner that is engaging and insightful. This book is timely given the sensitivity around the necessity of expanding light and discourse about the sexual expression of persons of African descent. Dr. Gilbert paves the way for scholars and practitioners with her work as *Black and Sexy* will be used in collegiate classrooms and lay communities for years to come. I wholeheartedly endorse this masterpiece and look forward to many conversations with my students. Bravo!

—**James C. Wadley**, Ph.D., CST-S; Editor in Chief of the Journal of Black Sexuality and Relationships, Lincoln University

"*Black and Sexy* does something other texts do not: It contextualizes race as not simply a social construct, but as a sexual social construct that white supremacy culture uses to pathologize the sexuality of African American and Afro-descended people. After naming the negative, traumatic roots of this framing, Dr. Gilbert brings the reader into a space of reconceptualization and healing, inviting Black individuals and communities to own, embrace and celebrate their sexuality. This should be required reading for all current and future sexologists."

—**Elizabeth Schroeder**, EdD, MSW; Sexuality Educator and Consultant

BLACK AND SEXY

A Framework of Racialized Sexuality

Tracie Q. Gilbert

NEW YORK AND LONDON

First published 2022
by Routledge
605 Third Avenue, New York, NY 10158

and by Routledge
2 Park Square, Milton Park, Abingdon, Oxon, OX14 4RN

Routledge is an imprint of the Taylor & Francis Group, an informa business

© 2022 Tracie Q. Gilbert

The right of Tracie Q. Gilbert to be identified as author of this work has been asserted by her in accordance with sections 77 and 78 of the Copyright, Designs and Patents Act 1988.

All rights reserved. No part of this book may be reprinted or reproduced or utilised in any form or by any electronic, mechanical, or other means, now known or hereafter invented, including photocopying and recording, or in any information storage or retrieval system, without permission in writing from the publishers.

Trademark notice: Product or corporate names may be trademarks or registered trademarks, and are used only for identification and explanation without intent to infringe.

Library of Congress Cataloging-in-Publication Data
A catalog record for this book has been requested

ISBN: 978-0-367-90058-8 (hbk)
ISBN: 978-0-367-90059-5 (pbk)
ISBN: 978-1-003-02218-3 (ebk)

DOI: 10.4324/9781003022183

Typeset in Joanna
by Apex CoVantage, LLC

CONTENTS

	Acknowledgments	ix
	Preface	xi
1	Introduction	1
	Understanding Sexuality: Why Race Matters	3
	Theories of Racialized Sexuality	4
	What Is Black Sexual Epistemology? A General Description	13
	Why *Black and Sexy*?	15
	Remaining Chapter Overview	16
2	Sexuality as "Sexiness Engineering"	21
	Toward Sexuality From Sexiness	23
	Erotic Beings, Erotic Selves	26
	The Control Panel—Exuded Being, Sensory Experience and the Eight Channels of Sexiness	28
	External Influences	30
	And What Of Race?	30
	Chapter Summary	32
3	Exuded Being	34
	Comportment	36

	Corporeality	40
	Performative Blackness	42
	Erotic Energy	45
4	**Sensory Experience**	**53**
	Sensual Pleasure	56
	Mental Excitation	61
	Relationship	64
	Positive Affect	70
5	**The Erotic Self**	**73**
	Doer/Be-er	75
	Journeyer	77
	Magnet	80
	Product	83
	Sexual Brand	85
6	**External Influences**	**89**
	Racial Maligning	91
	Commercialism	96
	Chronic Pain, Illness and Disability	98
	Sexual Trauma	99
	Sexual Precocity	101
	Technology	103
	Professional Identity	105
	BSE Model Summary	107
7	**BSE in Context—A Tool for Black Sexual Development**	**110**
	Contextualizing Blackness and Sexuality	111
	Race, Power and Sexuality Practitionership	112
	Theory Summary	115
	Proposing a Working Model of Black Sexuality/African American-Centered Sexual Development	117
	Intellectual/Research Implications	120
	Practitioner Implications	124
	Assumptions and Limitations	128
	Opportunities for Future Research	133
	Conclusion	135

Afterword	143
Appendices	155
Appendix A: BSE Research Study Methodology	157
Appendix B: Interview Schedule	173
Index	177

ACKNOWLEDGMENTS

I stand on the shoulders of amazing people. I am a product of their leadership, vision, innovation and undying support, for all of which I am grateful. There will, undoubtedly, be names that I miss while drafting this section. To those individuals, I apologize in advance. To all others, I send appreciation as follows.

To every scholar who has imagined the subject of racialized sexuality and its dimensions before me, including but not limited to Drs. Robert Staples, June Dobbs Butts, Abdul Jan-Mohammed, Joanne Nagel, Gail Wyatt, Gwendolyn Goldsby-Grant, Patricia Hill Collins, Kelly Brown Douglas, Nicholas Myers, E. Patrick Johnson, Herukhuti, Dionne Stephens and Layli Phillips, E. Christi Cunningham, Juan Battle and George Yancy, among countless others. I look up to you all and I marvel at the trails you've blazed, in that they've helped theorists like me to walk and speak more assuredly. I give thanks for my peers of the present moment: Drs. Candace Hargons and Shemeka Thorpe, Donna Oriowo, Lexx Brown-James, LaShay Harvey, Talena Queen and others—folks who raise the bar in academic scholarship and forge innovative new ways to tease out the converging factors of race and sex, particularly in the lives of Afro-descended people. I give thanks for this ever-evolving community and look forward to its continued growth and thriving.

To my dissertation committee, headed by the indomitable Dr. Donald Dyson and flanked by twin powerhouses Drs. Erika Evans and Twinet

Parmer, I thank you for your support, direction and, when needed, correction. For letting me "bite off more than I could chew," but giving me ample space, time and trust to digest it all, I am truly grateful. To every Black person—and particularly every Black femme—who pulled *extra* strings to make sure I had things I needed for this study to go off well (Shayla, Tanya and Sara—you're the BEST!), this final result is so much higher in quality (and less expensive!) having had you in my corner.

To all my colleagues in the field of human sexuality, including but not limited to the Women of Color Sexual Health Network and the Society of Black Scholars in Human Sexuality at Widener University: SALUTE! Your presence alone has been inspiring, and your consistent encouragement has been life-saving. You all are my comrades, and I don't take that lightly. THANK you for being your hopeful, unapologetic selves. To Clare Ashworth, Heather Evans, Upasruti Biswas and the entire team at Taylor & Francis, thank you for a) believing in this project and b) continuing to press your faith enough to make sure I completed this manuscript in a reasonable time frame!

To my family as a whole, but specifically my mother, Linda Jackson, and brother, Calvin Woodley: I love you both more than you will ever know. You remind me that no matter where I go, I always have a home to come back to and folks in that home who love me unconditionally. You two are MY LIFE. Thank you for being dope!

Finally, and most importantly, thank you to the 239 African Americans who answered my initial call to participate in this study, the 95 individuals who were interviewed and the dozens of sexuality practitioners and layfolk who've given audience to my thoughts since I first wrapped up my doctoral studies. This work is still first and foremost for YOU—for US! I remain amazed by your enthusiasm and for all you taught me about how we show up in the world. I will be forever grateful to you for your willingness to share yourselves with me and to ultimately see and encourage my vision. I pray this work serves as a powerful seed for game-changing insight into the Black sexual experience.

PREFACE

The following is a book about race, particularly about the ways that race and, by extension, racialization processes intersect with sexuality to inform the lives of African American people living in the United States. It discusses the specific theoretical framework of Black Sexual Epistemology, a name so given to represent the expressed articulations of the population under study. While this book is a direct offshoot of my dissertation research, my original motivation to write about sexuality and Black people came from initial studies as a master's student at the University of Pennsylvania, where I focused on sexuality development and African American adolescents. At the time my interests were less about sex and more about identity and other aspects of adolescent development at large; however, the addition of "Black" and "race" to my search terms at the time resulted in a deluge of comparative studies on sexuality between Black and other teens, in which Black teens were categorized as being the worst and most of all things categorized as problematic about sexuality and sexual health: unintended pregnancy, earlier sexual debut, increased reported partner history, etc.

What was perhaps most compelling about the bulk of data I consumed at that time was the lack of attention seemingly paid by researchers to the topic of race or racialization; that oversight is what pushed me further into exploring race and sexuality as a combined topic and, eventually, the former's influence on the latter. I would eventually go on to share additional thoughts on the matter during Widener University's 2011 Sex Ed Week in a presentation titled "Sexualized Racism & Racialized Sexuality: Historical and Ethical Perspectives"; this presentation has since evolved into a regular lecture I now facilitate on sexualized anti-Blackness in Western history. In this lecture I share quotes collected from such works as Thomas Gossett's *Race: The History of an Idea*, Dr. Joy DeGruy Leary's *Post Traumatic Slave Syndrome*, Harriet Washington's *Medical Apartheid: The Dark History of Medical Experimentation on Black Americans from Colonial Times to the Present* and Kelly Brown Douglas's *Sexuality and the Black Church: A Womanist Perspective*, illuminating the historical connection between race and sexuality in the U.S., while making the case for the through line I perceive between the racist sexual imagination of our nation's founding fathers and operationalized conceptions of sexuality in the present day.

In my work, racialization is best defined as "the process of being indoctrinated into a psychology and lived experience defined by skin color and/or other assigned cultural attributes." It is not predicated on whether an individual accepts this indoctrination or even if they resist or deny its existence—it is simply indicative of the process itself and how it operates. Despite my belief in the inextricability of race and sex within the American imagination, I realized early on that my assertion of this idea would be presumptive (and potentially harmful to the very communities my work is meant to serve) without cultivating solid evidence to support it. My desire to avoid this outcome led me to pursue my research agenda using the grounded theory method of qualitative research, which is ultimately how the present work was able to take form.

Grounded theory was most useful in this case for its ability to employ community voice in the generation of core ideas and concept interpretation. It might have been easier to design a study using preestablished race and sexuality-based theories or to rely on more phenomenologically based research designs; however, doing so would have fallen outside my original intention, perhaps even adding to the original anti-Blackness problem, because such research has historically been presumptive or problem-focused. Ultimately, the use of grounded theory allowed study participants to become co-creators in knowledge formation and interpretation—a position not consistently held among non-White populations in sexological research of the past.

It is useful to share some relevant details about my personal and professional background that lend credence to my being qualified to share this analysis. To begin, I completed four years of coursework at Widener University while a student in the Center for Human Sexuality Studies. I received a master's of education from the Center in 2014 in the area of human sexuality education, which trained me in the teaching of various aspects of human sexuality, including sexual diversity, sexual orientation and other subjects. This training was both cognitive and affective, with the latter part geared specifically toward increasing my capacity for discussing more sensitive aspects of the work. I have over a decade's worth of experience as a sexual health counselor, teacher and trainer, not including additional work I've done as a human sexuality professor at the undergraduate and graduate levels. To say I was always intellectually fascinated by sex is a bit of an understatement; one distinct memory I have from the 8th grade is of conducting interviews with all the boys on my school bus (all African American) about their sexual behavior and then recording their answers for my science teacher.

What I have learned from my studies thus far about the construction of sexuality seems to be more prescriptive than heuristic. For example, Dennis Dailey's Circles of Sexuality model was the first I was exposed to in this field, one that arguably dominates the professional discourse on "legitimate" aspects of sexuality. Yet while comprehensive in scope, his five circles have often felt antiseptic for me, seemingly incapable of drawing out the fullest extent of sexuality's role in everyday life. As a practitioner, I've found it additionally difficult to share the model clearly with Black and Latinx young people, often receiving blank stares (or, in extreme cases, vehement pushback) because they neither understand nor feel they can relate to the concepts within the model. As a whole, I am both intellectually fascinated by human sexuality and naturally inclined toward making otherwise lofty ideas accessible to a wide range of populations and intellectual levels. Writing this book was a natural progression from that aim.

The notion of "Black Sexuality" is not new in any sense of the word; one peek at any number of search engines would likely reveal a plethora of works to choose from, produced by academicians and layfolk alike. In comparison to those works, however, this offering emerges as a theoretical framework advanced through the lens of a sexuality educator—that particular bit of positionality signaling unique distinctions in not only what has been covered in the volume to follow but also its implications for future use and application. This work is "pracademic," with particular usefulness for those who do the work of assisting the world in understanding sexual concepts and ideas for their own personal lives and practices. And I make this last claim intentionally, in light of most recent calls across the profession of sex education to grapple with the history and contemporary practice of racial injustice within sex ed spaces. It is my hope that this work does not simply sit pretty on course syllabi in classes to be debated but is considered practically within this larger discourse for the purposes of advancing new conversations on the matter, even outside of what has been already offered.

To be sure, there are at least two different ways I believe racial justice can be achieved in sex education—and sexuality practitionership as a whole. For one, the history of reproductive harm that has been caused to Black and Brown communities is such that sex ed has not only the opportunity but also the responsibility to shed light on it so that it may be properly rectified. This includes introducing learners to historical experiences like the forced surgical experimentation performed on enslaved women Anarcha, Betsy, and Lucy by founding father of gynecology, Dr. J. Marion Sims, the Tuskegee Syphilis Study, the Puerto Rican contraceptive pill trials and, more recently, the forced sterilization of scores of Black and Brown women in the California prison system between the late 1990s and 2010s. Elevating stories like these and challenging educators to contend with the contemporary effects of this history assist with placing our work within its proper sociohistorical context while shedding light on the prevailing conscious and unconscious biases that continue to inform what is taught and how teachers show up in classrooms of color (especially for those who are LGBTQ+ identified), along with the persistent, justifiable mistrust and lack of safety often experienced by learners as a result.

Beyond this baseline, however, a truly racially just and equitable classroom, one that recognizes sexuality as both a normative and positive aspect of one's life and moves away from a solely health promotion narrative, has the opportunity to do more in the way of healing these injustices versus simply bringing them to light. Even when speaking of reproductive justice it is important to avoid wholesale conflation of it and racial justice, as while the former is rightfully concerned with the ways that systems of oppression directly impact the reproductive choices of Black and other child-bearing individuals, the procurement of all needed resources, technologies and schemas for ensuring healthy pregnancy and empowered reproductive choices for Black people will not alleviate the matter of racialization.

At the level of liberation, I believe sex ed pedagogy that is truly invested in racial justice can more effectively pursue it by using sex ed spaces to help audiences unpack the sexual harm and trauma caused by racism and racialization. This includes not only addressing education from a reproductive justice framework but also addressing the physiological and psychic violence that has been, for many, caused by anti-Blackness, White supremacy and their derivative ideologies. Diversifying traditional sex ed spaces by including more images and stories that feature people of color, even LGBTQ+ folks of color, is one thing; however, incorporating lessons that unpack and help learners heal and divest from practices like colorism/texturism, fatphobia, whorephobia, respectability politics, transmisogynoir and adultification of Black children is far more nuanced terrain for what is necessary and possible—terrain I anticipate frameworks like what I offer here can assist with traversing.

To conclude, I understand that this is a book that could rightfully be added to the current pantheon of writings about Black sexuality because of who it discusses and who is doing the discussing; in fact, I welcome this. This book, however, is slightly less about characterizing the sexuality of a people than it is about articulating the machinations of race and sexuality in the mind—not only for African Americans but also for society at large. As will be further articulated in the pages to follow, I invite and appreciate scholars of all communities to contend with the ideas presented here and to hopefully use them for further refection, debate and creation of new insights.

I thank you all.

Tracie Q. Gilbert, PhD
Thembi Anaiya, LLC

1

INTRODUCTION

In the fall of 2017 I began my dissertation by writing about the exclusion of Black people from *Playboy* magazine's 55 Most Influential People in Sex in the United States[1]—a list that even then was nearly ten years old yet was still just as intriguing to my mind less than a decade later. At the time, I was only somewhat clear about what such a faux pas could really mean, posing such questions to my own mind as, "Who would Elvis Presley be without Little Richard and Chuck Berry or Madonna without the NYC ball community?"—thinking specifically of included white popular entertainers whose artistry was directly influenced by Black originators. I struggled to understand who the people on the Top Ten list even were while also noting the lack of any of my own personal influences (Prince, Janet Jackson, Salt 'N' Pepa, Boyz II Men, to name a few) in the ultimate list. Beyond these questions, I also contended with at least one dissertation committee member who actively questioned how my focus on this pop culture oversight translated to my academic wish to address the overarching narrative of pathology applied to Black sexuality within sexology. What began as

DOI: 10.4324/9781003022183-1

surface critical inquiry ultimately became the present volume before you—an exposition on the ways that sex and race have influenced, and have thus been experienced by, African American people in the United States.

As it stands, there is no standard sexological text that expounds on the role of race in the sexual ideation/expression of African American people. While previous work exists that a) researches lived experiences or b) theorizes about Black sexuality more broadly, most have done so from a pathologizing framework, focusing predominantly on previously codified sexual problems versus amplifying normative or life-affirming experiences. There are several works outside of sexology that explore racialized sexuality; that said, none focus specifically on the schemas and structures involved in race and sexual ideation or expression or use extensive empirical data to support their ideas. From a cultural standpoint I believe this lends itself to the types of oversights I noted earlier—those of African American people who lend themselves to the advancement of sexual culture in America without getting their proper credit and acknowledgment. Academically, however, this also creates a significant gap in a field that has grown more aware over time of the intersectional challenges inherent to present sexuality practitionership and the need to divest from traditional sexological discourses that adversely affect those at the margins of gender, race, sexual orientation and the like. Indeed, a clarion call has sounded for all sexuality professionals to acknowledge that sexuality *and* race matter, yet some confusion still remains as to how race matters and to what degree—both quantitatively and qualitatively.

The premise of my book is simple enough. I assert that race is a sexual social construct that, when taken seriously within the context of sex education and sexuality practitionership, has the potential to offer clear insight into a path of healing and development for not just African American people, but for all people for whom race has been an identity marker over time. I specify the term *healing* for the specific purpose of elucidating another important point: that the average sexuality of an African American—or maybe even Black persons diasporically—cannot be fully understood without attending to the specific treatment of racialization provided by White supremacy and anti-Blackness. Evidence of such treatment abounds, with far too much depth and profundity to be fully detailed here. To quote Black studies scholar Greg Thomas most succinctly, however, "The entire history of our African presence in American captivity lays bare a raw sexual terror that defines the cult of white supremacy here and elsewhere" (1).[2] What I will attempt to do within the remaining chapters of this book is to, with bits and pieces of stories I've collected through my own work, shed light on the specific impact of this history on the contemporary sexual psyche of African Americans while offering some baseline ideas for how sexuality practitioners might incorporate this consideration into more effective work in these particular communities.

Understanding Sexuality: Why Race Matters

Race has come to be well understood in the present day as a social construct, only biologically significant to the degree that skin color diversity has corresponded with historical geographic migration patterns and environmental adaptations over time. Indeed, the social construction of race has had overwhelming salience in the organization and maintenance of American social life. Drs. Audrey and Brian Smedley have detailed the extent to which race has been socially organized in the U.S., adding that

> from a policy perspective, although the term *race* is not useful as a biological construct, policymakers cannot avoid the fact that social race remains a significant predictor of which groups have greater access to societal goods and resources and which groups face barriers—both historically and in the contemporary context—to full inclusion.
>
> (22)[3]

This can be clearly seen in the case of sexual health policy, as African American communities continue to face significant disparities when compared with other groups in this regard. Whether it be historical instances of systemic/generational poverty post-slavery and Jim Crow, contemporary instances of job and housing insecurity among Black LGBTQ+ individuals, limited access to high-quality and affirming community-based facilities or cost-prohibitive contraceptive and medication access, much of the overwhelming levels of African American representation within adverse sexual health outcome statistics can be attributed to persistent race- and gender-based economic inequalities.

That said, race and sexuality are not, as many contemporary sexuality scholars might assume, the substance solely of racist actions or policies enacted against darker-skinned bodies and communities by lighter ones. The presence of even the most advanced medical centers and affordable health technologies cannot make up for attending professionals who, for example, operate under false stereotypes about Black women's ability to tolerate pain or lack competence in identifying when Black babies need comfort or assistance. For this reason, it is important to note that at its core race informs not only the social and political power structures in the U.S. but also the psychological and psychic ones. Through its various social machinations it has served to essentialize physical, psychological and—by extension—sexual/erotic ways of being, routinely demarcating various populations from others based on assumed cultural and behavioral norms relative to skin color and teaching said groups how to see themselves and others in kind. It is this process of conscious–subconscious functioning with which the present volume is concerned, as it is this pervasive, insidious dynamic that creates the most important barrier for us as sexuality practitioners to overcome in the advancement of sexual wellness and healing for African American people.

Theories of Racialized Sexuality

What I will share in the next few chapters of this book is, in many ways, an empirical case supporting an operationalization of the construct of racialized sexuality. It is born from a constructivist grounded theory I created describing the lived experience of sexuality among African Americans in the present day. Though I have found no definite originator of the term that I am aware of, several scholars provide ample theory and description to effectively articulate how racialized sexuality has functioned over time. I share a few below as a framework for better understanding the emergent model of sexuality I propose. Sociologist Joane Nagel punctuates a portion of the first chapter of her book *Race, Ethnicity, and Sexuality: Intimate Intersections, Forbidden Frontiers* with the following:

> [d]espite the visceral power of sexual matters in general, especially those involving race, ethnicity, or the nation, the connection between ethnicity and sexuality often is hidden from view. Sex is the whispered subtext in spoken racial discourse. Sex is the sometimes silent message contained in racial slurs, ethnic stereotypes, national imaginings, and

international relations. Although the sexual meanings associated with ethnicity may be understated, they should never be underestimated.

(2)[4]

Such forms the basis of her theory of ethnosexuality, a conceptualization for imagining race and sexual intersections—particularly the sexual boundaries maintained within them over time. Nagel's primary assertion is that racial ideologies, by way of ethnic difference, will often correspond to sexual ideologies like these when diverse groups cohabitate a space. These ideologies emerge when groups are socially pitted against each other in an "us" versus "them" socialization process that reifies notions about each group's relative level of sexual morality or perversion. Extended further, Nagel argues that constructions of race within this framework cannot be fully understood when separated from constructions of sexuality. Within these "ethnosexual frontiers," as she calls them, the two become automatically fused, as racial identities become laden with untested, often (as in the case of African and other non-white peoples) hyper-negative sexual projections.

Several scholars have expounded the various stereotypical attributes European settlers used to describe African people upon their first encounters with each other (Brown Douglas, 1999; DeGruy Leary, 2005; Parmer & Gordon, 2007; Roberts, 1997; Staples, 2006; Stephens & Phillips, 2003). What is most relevant to this analysis is that a sizeable number of these projections directly speculated about African people's sexual nature (Brown Douglas, 1999; Gossett, 1963; Nagel, 2003). For example, "lustful" was one of the many negative adjectives included in the "scientific" classification of Black people in the 18th century (DeGruy Leary, 2005), and "in simiae" (in comparison to apes) was a term employed by some medical professionals to describe the penises of Black men, asserting them to be consistently larger than those of other men and even longer than their own bodies (Gossett, 1963). African women were not exempt from this treatment, as "Jezebel," reminiscent of the biblical figure known for her sexual looseness, was a common term used to describe them (Roberts, 1997).

In the case of the United States, Nagel (2003) argues that sexual morality has been historically considered as inherent an aspect of Whiteness as lasciviousness has been of non-Whiteness, and that to consider the ethnicity of either would be to automatically factor in this moral judgment. The most salient aspect of this perspective is that historically combined notions of White superiority and non-White inferiority grew to become instituted in most American social mores, including those related to the sexual behaviors of its citizens. Opinions about Black sexuality came to make up the narrative that helped embed intellectualized racism deeper in the fabric of U.S. public life and reverberate it back out to other parts of the world (DeGruy Leary, 2005; Nagel, 2003). It is this ideology that is said to ultimately serve as the foundation for sociohistorical—and particularly sexual—treatment of Black bodies, perpetuating present-day distinctions between African Americans and other ethnic groups (Parmer & Gordon, 2007; Smedley & Smedley, 2005). As a theory, then, ethnosexuality offers a useful baseline for imagining the ideology informing Black sexuality in the U.S.

Of all sexological theorists in history, sociologist Michel Foucault (1978) offers the most popular blueprint for identifying and articulating sexuality's social construction and function. With regard to society and its institutions, he asserts that sexuality emerges predominantly as a product of power, specifically expressed through overlapping social forces working simultaneously to shape its narrative and reinforce hierarchical rules of engagement (Foucault, 1978). Though not intentionally collaborative at the onset, sequential social norms established and maintained through interpersonal relationships within local institutions—townships, schools, churches, families and so on—serve, he argues, to legitimize and reify these overarching norms (Foucault, 1978). From this matrix, Foucault suggests that sexuality be best conceptualized as

> an especially dense transfer point for relations of power . . . not the most intractable element in power relations, but rather one of those endowed with the greatest instrumentality . . . capable of serving as a point of support, as a linchpin, for the most varied strategies.
>
> (103)

In this way, sexuality can be seen conceptually as a mechanism for the implicit, systematic control of sexual bodies and behaviors via the explicit negotiation and reification of socially established sexual norms, outside of any actual coital behaviors occurring among those being regulated (Weeks, 1985).

Foucault's overarching theory, the "repressive hypothesis," ultimately implicates institutions as "bourgeoisie" mobilized against any actions, including sexual, having a chief aim of pleasurable fulfillment. This idea becomes more intriguing when intersected with race—an analysis Foucault never provides yet is offered two-fold by colonial studies scholars Ann Stoler and Abdul JanMohamed. Stoler (1995) speaks directly to Foucault's omission of race in his original analysis when asking the following regarding the four "objects of knowledge" used in his imagining of bourgeoisie sexuality:

> [d]id any of these figures exist as objects of knowledge and discourse in the nineteenth century without a racially erotic counterpoint, without reference to the libidinal energies of the savage, the primitive, the colonized—reference points of difference, critique, and desire?
> (6–7)

Citing examples from the Dutch, French and English societies of the time, Stoler highlights a pattern in which European societies explicitly called upon the perceived sexual virtue of "whiteness" to delineate between those deemed authentic citizens of the state and those who were not. While much of Foucault's original ideas focused specifically on Europe's geographical borders, Stoler asserts that said ideologies did not end there and extended further west into the New World (Stoler, 1995). Her reworking of Foucault's analysis suggests two important ideas: that the advancement of bourgeoisie sexual discourse was tied to an implicitly white European advancement of empire, and that said advancement occurred in direct response to fears about the moral decline of an unchecked sexual society—ideas generated directly from racist projections about non-white European populations (Stoler, 1995). Moreover, Stoler's analysis charts a direct pathway from traditional imperialist ideas made about "primitive" Africans on their continent to colonial positions advanced against "savage" Native and African bodies in the Americas, setting up the aforementioned ethnosexuality elucidated by Nagel.

Race-related critiques of Foucault are not only focused on its placement within the time line of his analysis; JanMohamed and Stanton (1992) challenge Foucault's assertion that power is universal and shifting, available to all manner of human interaction, by arguing that such ideology has inherently precluded African Americans by virtue of their historically powerless position in American society. To be clear, they are not as concerned with what Foucault calls the "general equivalent of exchange" engendered by his emphasis on power as "the moving substrate of force relationship, . . . [that] by virtue of their inequality, constantly engender states of power," as much as they are with understanding how power "can be syphoned off, like surplus value, and how it comes to be *accumulated in institutional forms*, like capital" (JanMohamed & Stanton, 1992, 95–96, emphasis mine). This perspective is significant for the ways it directly rebuts Foucault's desire to move away from a "juridico-discursive" understanding of power when discussing sexuality by clarifying the ways that African American sexual expression has, in fact, been explicitly repressed and legislated against by powers of the state.

Historical legislation in the U.S. against miscegenation, or the sexual or romantic commingling of individuals of different racial backgrounds, is a major aspect of JanMohamed and Stanton's argument, though they, too, cite slave rape laws and slave marriage regulations as part of this history. "Juridical prohibitions are extremely powerful in this space," the authors note,

> because all socio-political-cultural relations on the racial border are predicated on the definition of the "other," in this case the [African] American, as nonhuman, as a being who does not belong to the human realm of the master's society and who subsequently has no "rights" within that society.
>
> (97)

JanMohamed and Stanton accurately identify each element of Foucault's juridico-discursive power construct as part and parcel of the African American historical experience, such that Foucault's final premise regarding universal human treatment in industrialized societies becomes theoretically limited. What the pair subsequently elucidate is a potential alternative answer to the question of how specific local power relations work in advancing a unique "racialized sexuality" for African Americans in the United States—one predicated on the motive of maintaining established differentiation of power between whites and non-whites.

George Yancy (2008) brings notions of racialized sexuality to the interpersonal and intrapsychic through his supposition of dynamics at play in the daily navigation of anti-Blackness[5] by Black people. As he explains it, Black people come to bear the brunt of anti-Black racism when making any attempts to assert themselves in ways contrary to the imposed white "imago" of Blackness, such that both their self-imagined and real selves are rejected and "returned back" to them with depictions falling more in line with anti-Black expectations (Yancy, 2008). The strength of this dynamic comes from the ingrained nature of the narrative. Among many others, including his own, Yancy cites an especially poignant example from Ralph Ellison's *Invisible Man* (1952) to support his claim—a particularly relevant exchange between the protagonist and a white woman character with fantastical notions about his sexual nature:

> Sybil wants him to take her against her will, to play at being raped by a Black "buck." . . . "You can do it. It'll be easy for *you*, beautiful. Threaten to kill me if I don't give in. You know, talk rough to me beautiful . . ." In a state of mythopoetic frenzy (and masochistic frenzy) she says, "Come on, beat me, daddy—you—you big black bruiser. What's taking you so long?" she said. "Hurry up, knock me down, don't you want me?" Annoyed, he slaps her, but this only leaves her "aggressively receptive." He never rapes her, but constructs the moment with a different semiotic spin, writing on her belly with lipstick: "SYBIL, YOU WERE RAPED BY SANTA CLAUS, SURPRISE."
>
> (Yancy, 2008, 77–78)

In this example, the protagonist is persistently thrown back an ethnosexual self-concept that is not of his design and becomes subject to rules of exchange that are directly beholden to the chimera that has been exerted. He is never able to define the parameters of who he will be in the moment, nor avoid his white companion's authority to pin him to her violent, hypersexualized projections. On a related note, it is telling that the white woman in this passage codes the protagonist as a rapist and not, as another possibility, a tender, romantic love of a lifetime; it is his Black skin and body that Yancy argues limit his ability to be imagined beyond anything other than a sexual menace, albeit a sexually desired menace in the moment but a menace nonetheless. What Yancy elucidates is a subjective historicity of blackness, threaded into the cultural landscape of Europe generally (and America), through which self-determined Black people ontologically disappear, replaced by a subjective white "chimera" (Yancy, 2008, 99) of anti-Blackness.

Yancy evokes W. E. B. DuBois's notions of "double consciousness" in his suggestion that anti-Blackness is responsible for creating a cognitive schism in Black people when attempting identity autonomy (Yancy, 2008). Specifically, he notes that

> having one's Black body returned as ontologically problematic, one begins to think, to feel, to emote, even if unconsciously: "Am I a nigger?" The internalization of the white gaze [by Black people] creates a doubleness within the Black psyche, leading to a destructible process of superfluous self-surveillance and self-interrogation.
>
> (68)[6]

In *Black Skin, White Masks*, Frantz Fanon (1952) adds further to this analysis by suggesting that anti-Blackness and its machinations have both necessitated and perpetuated a reactive Black community in constant search of Whiteness (with whiteness representing, in this case, sexual morality) to distance itself from, if not rid itself of, its internalized anti-Black fate. Under this construction, Black people globally, and African Americans by extension, lose their agency for self-definition and remain beholden to the whims of white social norms for legitimacy, relevance, thriving and survival.

Not all theories of racialized sexuality end in naming or describing racialized sexual phenomena. Sexologist Aih Djehuti Herukhuti Khepera Ra Temu Seti Amen (Williams, 2007) points a way toward sexual healing in Black communities by using a "theorizing" framework centered on the open articulation of sexual expressions that serve to challenge contemporary expectations about how Black bodies should exist and perform. Afrocentric Decolonizing Queer Theory (ADQT)—the official name of Herukhuti's framework—emerges from the premise that there exists a pervasive culture of silence and norm of erotophobia within many African American communities, advanced as a means to avoid judgment or bypass addressing the unacknowledged pain of history. "Black Funk," however, is the mechanism of ADQT that pushes back on this dialogical repression; it is both a physical space developed by Herukhuti for the purposes of helping Afro-descended bodies work through their respective challenges and a conceptual model for sexual liberation within Black communities and relationships. Herukhuti describes the function and benefit of Black Funk as follows:

> Black Funk created me through the preparation of my soul gestating in the black primordial waters of the Great Mother. Black Funk stirred the love, lust, passion, and cravings of my mother and father to desire each other, to want to taste each other's sun-baked flesh. . . . Their sex, Black Funk, provided the conduit through which my soul re-entered this world to produce my life's purpose. . . .
> . . . I believe that the healing, liberating, and rejuvenating resources we need for the planet and ourselves are restored within Black Funk. So I return to the funk, the Black Funk, in an effort to reclaim, affirm, and resurrect my birthright—to live, to love, and to learn.
> (14–15)[7]

According to Herukhuti, honest dialogical engagement with one's sexual desires, hindrances and proclivities creates a "conjuring" effect through which healing from the vestiges of the past can begin. Black Funk draws heavily from a foundation of erotic theory put forth by Audre Lorde (1985) as well as critical Afrocentric and Queer Theory.

As will be shown in parts through the remainder of this book, African Americans have experienced adverse effects from the anti-Blackness they have experienced through the process of American racialization. What will also be shown, however, is that this experience has not, and does not, signal a definite end to the possibilities of Black sexual expression. Indeed, it highlights whole ways that those affected continue to thrive and grow, and express the capacity to thrive and grow, despite the external adverse influences placed upon them. Along with the dialogical imperative advanced by Black Funk, the possibilities inherent within E. Christi Cunningham's (2010) wholism theory provide a solid framework for both thinking through the effects of history and addressing them in real time. From a wholist perspective, it is a given that Black sexuality is, though has not always been, conceptually bounded by anti-Blackness/White supremacy. This constriction is perceived to exist at multiple levels, including the cultural, affective, physical and genetic/physiological. Successfully remembering this trauma and unpacking its effects, Cunningham argues, is a key process in facilitating communal healing and development.

To be clear, however, remembering is not intended for its own sake and does not end at merely deconstructing trauma. Rather, Cunningham draws on the ideas of Toni Morrison to suggest remembering as a creative process ("re-membering") in which present-day Black people reenact cognitive and affective linkages to their ancestors' experiences, "living it over and over again, searching it, *confronting its danger, creating space for its rage, releasing the loss, and migrating into a whole and consistent present*" (38, italics mine).[8] Sexuality is employed as a useful strategy in re-membering; about this, Cunningham continues with the following:

> [s]exuality, including material sex, acts of expression, and gender and orientation, is a creative energy. Sexuality provides a specific example of the synergism of memory and identity. It represents a confluence of sexual memory (genetic, body, and cultural) of individuals and communities affecting a confluence of sexual identity (genetic, body, and cultural) of individuals and communities . . . sexuality shapes individual and communal identity through sexual memory. One possible result of some forms of sexuality is a rebirth or re-creation of identity as something new and whole. Sexuality, therefore, constitutes a powerful ritual re-membering.
>
> (39)[9]

Wholism appears to potentially pair well with Black Funk as dual mechanisms in which the processes of healing and self-reclamation can be engaged. *Sexiness development*—a concept about which I will expound further along in a future chapter—is an example of sexual existence that can be seen or utilized by African American people as a means of re-creation—of reclaiming positive sexual ideation outside of conventional hegemonic norms and of creating new sociocultural memories, restoring affirmed erotic selves and healing ancestral trauma present within their genomic structures.

Cunningham defines wholism as a process in which Black identity creation occurs "out of bounds" or divorced from hegemonic constraints exerted against the community. This hegemony emerges through at least three avenues: dominant oppression, nondominant oppression and self-limitation. In speaking about how the second avenue emerges within contemporary Black sexual discourses, Cunningham notes that "[n]ormalized nondominant sexual identity is heterosexual and may be Black. Queer sexualities either do not exist or are products of 'the white man's' influence" (50).[10] This idea is an example of those noted earlier about sexual policing that occurs both intraculturally and between cultural groups. If there is any norm stressed within the wholism theory, however, it is that of diversity; within this conceptualization, an ideal or whole sexual self is one that is particular to the individual, unbound by any logic other than that gained from one's own journey and its resonance with ancestral truths. This aspect appears critical to the theory, as it avoids reifying norming processes that recreate trauma for marginalized emergent sexualities.

What Is Black Sexual Epistemology? A General Description

Several theories and models have appeared over time describing the effects of racialized sexualization on African American people in the present day. As stated earlier, however, there is limited to no sexological research that is intentional about understanding normative African American sexual experiences from an African American psychological perspective (Staples, 2006). Of the works that do exist, few to none have been conducted by sexologically trained generalists or explicitly consider the subject of racialization. Additionally, a number of those that are written by sexologists are considerably outdated (30-plus years old), limited by changes in technological influence, globalization, generational shifts and social attitudes overall (Staples, 1981). Though some changes can be seen within the past five years, many works presently available from African American sexologists are hindered by their own limiting aspects, including myopic focus, bits of unsubstantiated theorizing and even outright sex negativity and sexuality policing. The present work centers on a middle-range theory I call Black Sexual Epistemology (BSE); it extends from those outlined earlier to directly employ African Americans in an articulation of what the history of racialization and anti-Blackness has meant to their sexuality in the present day.

Black Sexual Epistemology describes a process that begins within the mind of a sexual engineer, or Erotic Self; this energy is the agentic center of all erotic beings, regardless of their level of sexual activity. Erotic Selves move about the world participating in sexual encounters that aid in the development of their "sexiness," operationalized as Exuded Being or Sensory Experience. The development of sexiness, while not always achieved, is almost always intended with one's sexual expression, as doing so aids in the advancement of self-mastery and fulfillment. The process of exuding and experiencing through the senses is expressed through up to eight distinct energetic channels and, at times, moderated by External Influences, including those related to race. Collectively, these elements and the resulting ways they interact with each other establish the erotic universe that is sexuality.

BSE is a constructivist grounded theory whose elements may be salient for other groups yet specifically centers African American people and most clearly articulates African American and, potentially, African diasporic cultural experiences. My goal for conducting the research supporting this model was to present a comprehensive theory of normative Black sexuality that not only included African American voices but also based itself directly on their words and ideas, allowing them to be co-creators in the knowledge generation process. I began with the term "sexiness" as a base concept, asking people to describe, define and articulate sexiness as they understood it, with the goal of making a definitive etymological link from there to sexuality at large (from sexi-"ness" to sexual-"ity," aka "the state or condition or quality of sex"). As much as was sensible, I used exact words and terminology presented by my target audience along with exact, verbatim interpretations of these ideas. While I was unable to make an equivalent link, I was able to gather from the data what sexiness looked like phenomenologically, working from there to make the link to sexuality relationally. Ultimately, then, this is a theory of both epistemological and ontological knowledge and describes themes and concepts that may be useful to explaining both constructs and processes accessed by the target population.

Though it is not prescriptive, the resultant theory is offered as a foundation for engaging in speculative discourse about best practices for facilitating knowledge, skill and attitude growth for both the population and those who wish to serve them. In addition, it offers a poignant question for deeper consideration: "what might Black sexuality look like without anti-Blackness/White supremacist interference?" While I would not dare assert to have answered this question in this present volume, I do believe that the information unpacked might still be useful for articulating an alternate imagining of Black sexuality that is rooted in vitality, resilience and resistance.

Why *Black and Sexy*?

This offering is admittedly as much personal as it is professional. I am an African American researcher who has worked as a sexual health counselor, educator and trainer for nearly a decade, the bulk of that time with African American young people living in urban settings. With few periodic exceptions, the bulk of my school age, high school and undergraduate years was also spent in segregated spaces with other African Americans, including the current town I live in, in which there is mostly Black leadership. I have had a natural curiosity about sex for most of my life and have been keenly sensitive to its expression in my culture of origin and home community. My understanding of sexuality as a child was informed as much by the media I was exposed to (Black family sitcoms on television and R&B, soul and rap music from African American performers, often featuring implicit and explicit sexual content) as by messages I received from caring yet stereotyping adults in my life. Sex was never discussed in my house or school; however, two implicit messages I remember receiving from that upbringing were a) sex was a good, "sexy" experience and b) sex was for adults only. It was that schema that would result in my waiting until I was 21 years old before experiencing my coital debut despite the common labeling of adults in my community as being "at risk" and the common teasing I received from peers about the likelihood of "wildin' out" once I left high school and went to college.

My sexual upbringing is at least partially informed by religion; however, religious doctrine was not as strong of an influence on my sexual phenomenology prior to my undergraduate studies even though my family and I were regular churchgoers before then. Attending an Historically Black College in the South is what exposed me to a more conservative Christian ethos about sex; it was where I learned about concepts like "soul ties," or the belief that sex before marriage could create unhealthy spiritual bonds that destroy a person mentally and emotionally. I would argue, however, that even that experience was informed by Blackness, particularly the respectability politics involved in growing into a professional Black woman who could avoid "becoming a statistic." All in all, I am of the clear belief that my sexual upbringing was predominantly, if not completely, racialized, which is to say that it was informed by and extended directly from my identity experience as a queer-identified, cisgender Black woman from a working class urban community.

Choosing *Black and Sexy* as the title of this book is both a play on the concepts discussed in the BSE model and a love letter to my proximal and distal community of origin. In my estimation, there is a certain vibrancy inherent to African American and other Afro-descended cultures—our music, language, food, fashion, behavior, etc.—that has consistently felt unaddressed by the simplicity of present sexological discourse yet presents like nothing less than, for lack of a better term, "sexual" at its core. Not sexual in the copulative sense, necessarily, but sexual in the sense of constituting the same type of energetic interaction that copulative activity might elicit. In hindsight, I realize that I was as much—if not more—interested in unpacking and naming this ideology through my research as I was in addressing anti-Blackness, as I believe it to be an interwoven yet underdiscussed aspect of both African American/Afro-descended cultures and sexuality itself.

Ultimately, my experiences and particular upbringing engendered in me a deep love and appreciation for where I come from as well as for those I perceive to be from my same cultural group. I entered this project committed to creating a work that would directly benefit Afro-descended people, or at least provide a foundation for them to be better served by the sexology field. That positionality combined with the formal skills I have gained in conducting qualitative research served as the foundation for effective completion of this study.

Remaining Chapter Overview

Black and Sexy consists of seven chapters that cover the entirety of the Black Sexual Epistemology model and its components. The first chapter was used as a means to establish race as the sexual social construct warranting its study in the ways that will follow. Chapter 2 lays out a more in-depth description of the BSE model, extending from the concept of Sexuality as "sexiness engineering." It reviews each of BSE's components in more depth and then sets up Chapters 3 through 6, which include stories of the nearly 100 African Americans who were interviewed for this study. In the seventh and final chapter of this work, I share thoughts and reflections on BSE's significance to the present time along with concrete ideas for how it can be incorporated and expanded on by sexual practitioners to improve the quality of the work we do.

To add an increased sense of personality to this work, I've included a collection of stories that introduce Chapters 2 through 6. These stories are not of real people; however, some elements of these stories do come directly from respondents along with other individuals whose stories I've come across in both professional and personal circles. I present each of them here as a way to set up their respective chapters and as even fuller examples of the kinds of people whose experience might be served and represented by the BSE theoretical framework. With the sum total of African American sexual treatment under consideration, it should be no surprise that healing is a major theme within some, if not most, Black sexological discourse (Cunningham, 2010; Wyatt, 1997). If African Americans are inundated with the regular toxicity of inaccurate messaging about what they do with their bodies and, by extension, what those behaviors mean, it follows that there might be deleterious effects warranting a response intended to bring about reconciliation. It is my firm belief that models like BSE can be useful for ushering in this process more efficiently and with greater lasting impact.

Notes

1 Radosh, D. (2009, January 13). The biggest names in sex. The Daily Beast. Retrieved from www.thedailybeast.com/the-biggest-names-in-sex
2 Thomas, G. (2007). *The sexual demon of colonial power: Pan-African embodiment and erotic schemes of empire.* Bloomington, IN: Indiana University Press.
3 Smedley, A., & Smedley, B. D. (2005). Race as biology is fiction, racism as a social problem is real: Anthropological and historical perspectives on the social construction of race. *American Psychologist,* 60(1), 16–26. https://doi.org/10.1037/0003-066x.60.1.16
4 Nagel, J. (2003). *Race, ethnicity, and sexuality: Intimate intersections, forbidden frontiers.* New York: Oxford University Press.
5 Other scholars have written about *anti-Blackness* and have advanced their own theoretical definitions of the term (Brady, 2014). Borrowing from the work of sociologist João Costa Vargas (2008), I define it here as the sociopolitical, psychological organizing of Afro-descended people around/via the narrative of death for the purpose of their physical and socioemotional demise—a definition inspired by the UN 1948 definition of genocide.

I find this definition of *anti-Blackness* useful for the ways it also sets up a consideration of the socioemotional toll genocidal actions against Black people take on the psyche of both recipients and initiators. Extending several steps conceptually from racism, anti-Blackness is both a physical and "paradigmatic" phenomenon, inextricably linking Blackness and death in human consciousness, to the point that they become wholly synonymous (Brady, 2014). What emerges from racialized sexuality when the lens of anti-Blackness is applied is a type of subjective Blackness that is rooted in marginalization, degradation, retardation and violence. Even among those who are physically alive, the result is an emergent "zombie-like" status through which one's lived experiences, including sexuality and one's sexual identity and relationships, become filtered.

6 Yancy, G. (2008). *Black bodies, white gazes*. Lanham, MD: Rowman & Littlefield Publishers.
7 Williams, H. (2007). *Conjuring black funk: Notes on culture, sexuality, and spirituality* (Vol. 1). New York: Vintage Entity Press.
8 Cunningham, E. C. (2010). Creation out of bounds: Toward wholistic identity. In Battle, J., & Barnes, S. L. (Eds.), *Black sexualities: Probing powers, passions, practices, and policies* (Ch. 2). New Brunswick, NJ: Rutgers University Press.
9 Cunningham (2010).
10 Cunningham (2010).

References

Brady, N. (2014). *Riding with death: Defining anti-blackness*. Retrieved from https://progressivepupil.wordpress.com/2014/02/27/right-to-death-defining-antiblackness/

Brown Douglas, K. (1999). *Sexuality and the black church: A womanist perspective*. Maryknoll, NY: Orbis Books.

Costa Vargas, J. H. (2008). *Never meant to survive: Genocide and utopias in black diaspora communities*. Lanham, MD: Rowman & Littlefield Publishers.

Cunningham, E. C. (2010). Creation out of bounds: Toward wholistic identity. In Battle, J., & Barnes, S. L. (Eds.), *Black sexualities: Probing powers, passions, practices, and policies* (Ch. 2). New Brunswick, NJ: Rutgers University Press.

Degruy Leary, J. (2005). *Post traumatic slave syndrome*. Milwaukie, OR: Uptone Press.

Ellison, R. (1952). *Invisible man*. New York: Random House. Cited in Yancy, G. (2008). *Black bodies, white gazes*. Lanham, MD: Rowman & Littlefield Publishers.

Fanon, F. (1952). *Black skin, white masks*. New York: Grove Press.

Foucault, M. (1978). *The history of sexuality* (Vol. 1). New York: Vintage Books.

Gossett, T. F. (1963). *Race: The history of an idea in America*. New York, NY: Oxford University Publishers.

JanMohamed, A. R., & Stanton, D. C. (1992). Sexuality on/of the racial border: Foucault, Wright and the articulation of "racialized sexuality". In *Discourses of sexuality: From Aristotle to AIDS*. Ann Arbor, MI: University of Michigan Press.

Lorde, A. (1985). Uses of the erotic: The erotic as power. In *Sister outsider*. Freedom, CA: The Crossing Press.

Nagel, J. (2003). *Race, ethnicity, and sexuality: Intimate intersections, forbidden frontiers*. New York, NY: Oxford University Press.

Parmer, T., & Gordon, J. J. (2007). Cultural influences on African American sexuality: The role of multiple identities on kinship, power, and ideology. In Tepper, M. S., & Owens, A. F. (Eds.), *Sexual health, Vol. 3: Moral and cultural foundations* (pp. 173–201). Westport, CT: Praeger Publishers/Greenwood Publishing Group.

Radosh, D. (2009, January 13). The biggest names in sex. *The Daily Beast.com*. Retrieved from www.thedailybeast.com/the-biggest-names-in-sex

Roberts, D. (1997). *Killing the black body: Race, reproduction, and the meaning of liberty*. New York: Vintage Books.

Smedley, A., & Smedley, B. D. (2005). Race as biology is fiction, racism as a social problem is real: Anthropological and historical perspectives on the social construction of race. *American Psychologist*, 60(1), 16–26. https://doi.org/10.1037/0003-066x.60.1.16

Staples, R. (1981). *World of black singles*. Westport, CT: Praeger.

Staples, R. (2006). *Exploring black sexuality*. Lanham, MD: Rowan & Littlefield.

Stephens, D. P., & Phillips, L. D. (2003). Freaks, gold diggers, divas, and dykes: The sociohistorical development of adolescent African American women's sexual scripts. *Sexuality & Culture*, 7(Winter), 3–49. https://doi.org/10.1007/bf03159848

Stoler, A. (1995). *Race and the education of desire: Foucault's history of sexuality and the colonial order of things*. Durham, NC: Duke University Press.

Thomas, G. (2007). *The sexual demon of colonial power: Pan-African embodiment and erotic schemes of empire*. Bloomington, IN: Indiana University Press.

Weeks, J. (1985). *Sexuality and its discontents.* New York: Routledge.
Williams, H. (2007). *Conjuring black funk: Notes on culture, sexuality, and spirituality* (Vol. 1). New York: Vintage Entity Press.
Wyatt, G. E. (1997). *Stolen women: Reclaiming our sexuality, taking back our lives.* New York: John Wiley & Sons, Inc.
Yancy, G. (2008). *Black bodies, white gazes.* Lanham, MD: Rowman & Littlefield Publishers.

2

SEXUALITY AS "SEXINESS ENGINEERING"

CALINDA'S STORY

Calinda is a 31-year-old single young woman from Indianapolis, Indiana; she currently lives and works as a veterinarian in Virginia. Growing up, sex was not really a major focus in Calinda's life. While she did have a few crushes she did not do any dating, as she was focused on following in her parents' footsteps to graduate from college and become a veterinarian. While her parents did not talk at all about sex, Calinda learned early on from leaders in her church, schoolteachers and administrators and afterschool program counselors that sex would "ruin her life," particularly if she did it before marriage and ended up pregnant. Even with the sexual urges she experienced in high school, Calinda made it a priority to focus on her studies, "do the right thing" and avoid becoming the statistic that was assumed about girls from her lower middle-class yet predominantly Black neighborhood. Calinda's efforts earned her a scholarship to a prestigious HBCU in the south, where she maintained a 3.8 grade point average while making the conscious choice to keep all serious relationships to a minimum. For Calinda this also meant continuing to avoid sex, as she did not want to get serious with anyone, risk getting distracted and jeopardize her future. (Note: while she had overheard various discussions about masturbation in her residence hall, she felt too embarrassed to look it up or ask anyone else about it.)

After graduation, Calinda thought she might be ready to become more sexually active. While she did start to date more, recurring thoughts of becoming "a single mother on welfare, with a deadbeat" kept her from going further in her sexual activity than general outercourse. The pressure to marry combined with her general discomfort with sex turned many of the potential suitors she met away. At present, Calinda feels the call even more urgently to date seriously, get married and begin having a more robust sex life. While she has learned some things about sex through groups and accounts she follows on social media, she doesn't know the first thing about how to initiate sexual encounters, nor about what she desires. What she knows for sure, however, is that she doesn't want to date anyone but a Black man since, in her mind, "Black Love is the pinnacle of everything," and "that's just who I'm attracted to." She would also rather not initiate a search for sexual partners because she doesn't want to come off as too aggressive or not submissive enough for the type of men she desires.

The aforementioned story and the others throughout the rest of this book are a small smattering of the kinds of experiences that live among those who might identify with Black Sexual Epistemology. BSE is a symbolic interactionist theory meant to describe and explain actors and elements involved within a particular social process. In this context, the theory expounds on specific elements that African American people use to conceptualize, engage in, make meaning of and thus shape their sexual experience. Robbins, Chatterjee and Canda (2006) define symbolic interaction as "the dynamic process of interaction between the person and the environment that results in a self that is continually growing and changing" (296)[1]. The fundamental position within BSE is that African Americans use sexuality to develop their sexiness—a ubiquitous, dynamic and universal yet personal process of fulfillment and self-mastery.

BSE draws from language used in recording and music technology to describe how individuals engage in various actions to develop and express their sexiness. Similar to a sound engineer in a recording studio, each individual possesses a "control panel" or mixing board, representing their body, mind, emotions, etc.—the hard- and software through which they process information. The control panel is an extension of the engineer (referred to in the BSE model as the Erotic Self), who possesses the bulk of control over what comes in and out of it. Control panels contain "channels" that facilitate the flow of sound to the places where it can be heard. As they move about in the world, sexiness is funneled through the channels of an engineer's control panels and is witnessed either by the engineer alone or simultaneously with others. Each channel in the BSE model represents a dimension of sexiness; sliders help determine the general "volume" at which each channel can be experienced. Channels can be experienced at low or high volumes, and volume levels can be determined by a number of factors, including the individual's awareness of the sonic possibilities present within that channel, their interest in utilizing the channel, their efforts to raise or lower the channel's signal frequency or other mitigating factors outside of their control.

The process of audio engineering typically involves mixing together chosen sounds—voice, music, sound effects—to create one overarching soundscape. This process is usually intentionally directed toward producing a specific end result, though in some cases it may be fairly random, proceeding more experimentally until a certain level of sonic satisfaction is achieved. Such is the same for sexiness, in that the engineer may intentionally seek to cultivate a particular experience of sexiness or sexiness development path. In other cases the individual may simply be experimenting, trying out different experiences for size and possibly even stumbling on sexual and sensual combinations they did not know were originally possible when they started. In an ideal mixing session, the engineer leaves with a high-quality recording of their soundscape that may then be used for a myriad of entertainment purposes. In the BSE model the Erotic Self and the individual's sexual engagement and sexiness are the high-quality recording, indicative of their resultant sexual expression.

Toward Sexuality From Sexiness

I began this study with specific interest in understanding sexuality through the lens of "sexiness." For each respondent I asked the question "What is sexiness to you?" with the hope of having respondents speak specifically to the definitive aspects of sexuality in their own mind. On its own, sexiness was a salient concept for respondents and is a cornerstone of the

BSE model. Sexiness is seen as a variable, "fluid" entity capable of change, growth and development. Its mercurial quality can be more immediate, as Leola describes ("when two individuals, or anyone, can just, I guess, flow with each other . . ."), or based on a range corresponding to the life cycle, as Ashton suggests ("[Y]ou experience [sexuality] literally from birth to death, so it's not something that, like, stops at one point and begins as another, you know what I mean? So it's on a long continuum."). It is precisely its capacity for providing growth and development that gives sexiness an aspirational quality to the individual. Indeed, sexiness is not only what is or can be; its perceived benefit also makes it something that is actively pursued or cultivated. As Doug, a heterosexual Ohio man in his 30s, described it, sexuality is

> a movement; you can't sit still with it. It's not something you can draw and say, like, "That's it." This one word, that's it. This one image, that's it. 'Cause I kinda see that in different people, when it comes to how they express their sexuality it's always . . . progressing. Or the opposite; some people are regressing.

Growth and development are an expected aspect of the sexiness process. Many of the individuals I interviewed either anticipated growing in their ability to exude or improve sensory experiences, perceived themselves to be in the midst of a particular growing experience or looked back with fondness on the ways in which they'd been able to grow in accessing and embracing sexiness over time. Because of this, participants were adamant that sexuality and sexiness, by extension, need space to grow:

> [s]exiness is something to me that can be very expansive. It's something that shouldn't necessarily be pigeonholed into a box of five or six things. I think it's something that can grow and can change and can evolve.
>
> (Cornell, personal communication)

To be clear, the pursuit of sexiness may involve "having sex," though it is not defined by coital activity. Moreover, cultivating opportunities for sexiness to be experienced is no guarantee that it will be. Individuals know that sexiness can vary from day to day or even moment to moment, sonically perfect on the best day or floating just above a whisper on the worst. When an individual has optimized their own exudation and sensory volumes—a task that, by most estimations, takes a lifetime—that is when full sexiness development has been achieved.

While everyone felt comfortable answering the question, most respondents' answers felt more descriptive in nature, corresponding to objects, behaviors, attitudes, etc., they deemed to be sexually attractive or to have sex appeal. Several respondents did provide more definitive responses to the question, though remarked at several points about their perceived difficulty in doing so. Coincidentally, the descriptions of sexiness respondents provided did appear to link to definitive accounts, allowing me to ultimately view them as branches of the same concept. For example, individuals who used definitive terms to answer the sexiness question defined it as being "the vibe a person is giving off," "something that you are" and "a feeling," while descriptive examples of sexiness like "confidence," "self-possession," "power" and "arousal" all appeared to represent examples of those definitive ideas. In both accounts, sexiness emerged as a type of attractive energy originating within a subject/object of attention, extending outward toward a recipient or observer and often becoming affiliated with a particular sensory experience. The concepts used in the BSE model to name these are Exuded Being and Sensory Experience.

Despite finding clear themes for codifying sexiness within the model, my original question did not appear reliable for defining sexuality on its own, which is why the two are related to one another in the BSE model but are not conflated (i.e., sexiness is established as a component of sexuality, though sexuality is not wholly constitutive of sexiness). While most respondents' answers would suggest that sexiness and sexuality are considered one and the same for many people, several other respondents begged to differ, identifying distinctions that proved helpful in distinguishing between the two. For example, Milan, a Philadelphia woman in her 30s, noted: "[sexuality] is a much broader term; it's . . . I feel like . . . it's not directly sexiness, it's like the whole aspect of sex, of all things entailed with that . . ." Vivi, a heterosexual woman in her late 30s, offered a more expounded perspective:

> the way I understand sexuality is a broad definition [and] is very subjective to each individual person. And so I think, for me, to say that these are things that are sexy to me? And there—they could be a component of someone's sexuality—meaning one person and then other people

possibly, but I think when I think of sexuality, I think of a broader experience, um, that would—the broader definition would apply differently to different people.

Broad was a common term used to describe the comparative qualities of sexuality among those who did not see it and sexiness as the same. Elle, a 20-something college student in Detroit, referred to sexuality as "this huge, many-armed beast of things and, you know, ideas and—and identities and wants and needs and like different people identifying in different ways . . ." She went further to assert that "I can experience sexiness, and I can be aroused and I can have sexual feelings and attractions, but, like, the grand conversation of, like, 'SEXUALITY' is . . . [it] just kinda exists outside of me." From this perspective, one might argue that sexuality is not an inherent quality of personhood. Doing so, however, would still beg the question of how to reconcile the ease with which others made such a cognitive connection.

Ginger Dee, a Delaware woman in her early 30s, offered the perspective that helped tie together the initial gaps between respondents who affirmed the connection and those who did not:

> I feel like my concept of sexuality is bigger than me. Like, it's bigger than my individual preferences. I feel like it's—*when I think of sexuality, I think of a global sense of, um, people maneuvering around each other* . . . and things that aren't specific to me as this one pinpoint in this larger constellation.
>
> (italics mine)

Being "one pinpoint in this larger constellation," as she put it, helps to establish sexuality as a theoretical universe in which sexiness is engineered. Returning to the sound engineering example, it is from this home base that we can imagine the entirety of an individual's soundscaping process—the control panel extending from one's erotic self, channels, mixing process and sexiness signal inputs and resultant high-quality recording—as the universe of Sexuality many have come to know.

Erotic Beings, Erotic Selves

In the BSE model erotic possibility is the foundation of one's sexual universe, which is to say that, like an instrument ready for use by its musician, sexiness can reside in an individual long before one ever becomes an Erotic Self. This makes all individuals—all entities, period—erotic beings, though not necessarily Erotic Selves. This is an important point to establish, as it explains the exuded being or sensory experience one might gain through interacting with an inanimate or nonhuman entity (e.g., paintings, music notes), as some respondents established in their responses. It also explains how, as other respondents noted, one might experience attraction from others without making any attempt on their part to enact them. Though linked to the same fundamental energy, Erotic Selves extend from erotic beings through the aspect of doing versus being, or intention versus inhabitance. Erotic Self refers to the personal locative quality named within respondents' descriptions of sexuality; to describe it simply as the sexiness engineer, however, is almost an understatement. More definitively, The Erotic Self is the agentic driving force impelling all that an individual is and does sexually. Within the BSE model the Erotic Self is the chief arbiter of all decisions made regarding the sexual soundscape one creates. No experience of sexiness can be achieved within any sexual universe without express agreement and coherence granted by the Erotic Self, which is a testament to the power it holds.

The idea of the Erotic Self emerged after participants were invited to answer the question "In what ways do you see yourself fitting within your understanding of sexuality?" While some considered themselves solely an aspect of the larger constellation of sexuality, as Ginger Dee described, many others asserted that defining sexiness was "a personal decision" that could not be automatically generalized to the next person. Indeed, the notion of Erotic Self emerged from the myriad ways sample respondents saw themselves within their own conceptualizations of sexiness and sexuality, along with the persistent assertion that sexuality "means different things to different people." This means then that while every Erotic Self has access to the same control panel and channel possibilities, each sexual soundscape created will ultimately reflect the unique combination of frequencies (i.e., exudations and sensory experiences) that are most desirable to the individual and to which they perceive themselves as having the most access. In practice, Erotic Selves may direct their engineering intentions toward others, seeking to use their exuded being to draw others in for cultivating sensory experiences. This is not required, however, with some Erotic Selves choosing to limit the degree of sensory experience they

28 SEXUALITY AS "SEXINESS ENGINEERING"

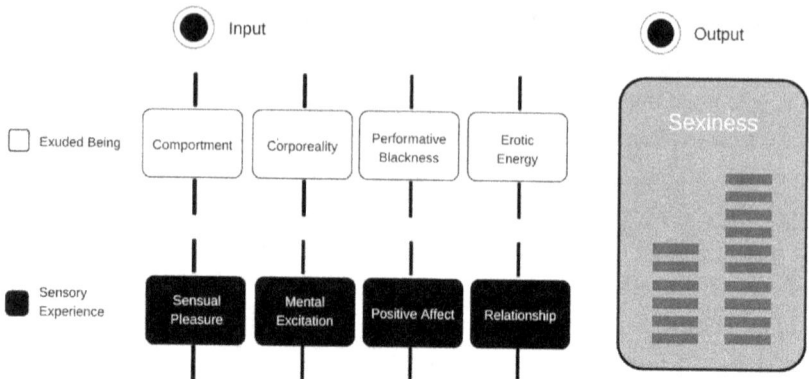

Figure 2.1 BSE: Eight Channels of Sexiness

engage in with others or forgoing external interactions altogether, focusing instead on the sensory experiences they cultivate within themselves. At no point is this process isolated, however, as it occurs in tandem with other Erotic Selves navigating their own control panels and sexiness engineering in kind. The collective combination of sexual universes serves to create the overarching constellation of Sexuality that is universal to all humankind.

A pictoral image representing the Eight Channels of Sexiness described in the BSE or Sexiness Engineering Model

The Control Panel—Exuded Being, Sensory Experience and the Eight Channels of Sexiness

Exuded Being and Sensory Experience serve as the two main emergent categories of sexiness within the BSE model. Roughly, these can be defined as the attractive energy, personal characteristics and other qualities given off (or "exuded") by an erotic being and the various experiences of the senses that occur as a function of that attraction. Exuded Being and Sensory Experience are significant for the ways that they facilitate sexiness development within an erotic being. Exuding a sense of self that is confident, aesthetically pleasing, empowered and capable of interacting well with others serves as the basis of personal satisfaction and self-mastery for most, if not all, respondents in the sample. In society, we may often be drawn to exuded beings for the sensory experience(s) they provide us—for example, inspiration, physical pleasure, intellectual stimulation or emotional safety/closeness. We may also be drawn to an exuded being for its perceived ability to lead to a desired future sensory experience—being attracted to a well-spoken person whom we subsequently wish to date, for example.

There are eight separate channels through which Exuded Being and Sensory Experience flow. Comportment, Corporeality, Performative Blackness and Erotic Energy are the four channels I've identified under Exuded Being. Sensual Pleasure, Mental Excitation, Positive Affect and Relationship make up the four channels of Sensory Experience. That sexiness can be imagined in such a comprehensive way represents the overwhelmingly vast diversity of answers provided by respondents to the question. Respondents discussed a wide range of character traits ("confidence," "self-love"), emotions ("safety," "joy," "love") and relational skill sets ("being calm") as part of their original answers to the "What is sexiness?" question. They described items of clothing, body parts, facial expressions, body language ("swagger"), activities and events. They talked about smells, tastes, colors, sounds, sights and physical sensations. They expounded on "energy," "life force" and the nature of spiritual attraction between masculine, feminine and beings in between. They name-checked celebrities (e.g., Beyoncé, Lizzo) and lauded specific behaviors exhibited in favorite songs and music videos. They applied critical eyes to the entire discussion, examining its political and commercial intersections ("Victoria's Secret"). And they often spoke of themselves and the ways in which they embodied or desired to embody sexiness for personal edification. As can be seen, individuals reported experiencing a whole host of "sounds" emerging through each of these channels, though the common thematic quality of exuded energy and sensory experience is what ultimately remained consistent throughout.

The channels of sexiness outlined here are not mutually exclusive. As will be shown, they can and often are modulated concurrently, depending on the context. Channel volumes can build and harmonize; however, the presence of volume on all channels is not required to achieve sexiness. While some channels appear more frequently within the data, they are not necessarily hierarchical in value and may all be present to varying degrees within the erotic self or encounter in question.

External Influences

Sexiness development does not occur without its fair share of interference; indeed, the ability to engage or fulfill sexual expression can be both strengthened and dampened by a host of factors within and outside of an individual's control. Within the BSE model, these aspects are called External Influences; in the audio engineering analogy they would be effectively referred to as "gain," or the increase/decrease in the strength of a signal as it goes through its respective channel. In an ideal world, Erotic Selves successfully navigate their sexuality by expressing and accessing Exuded Being and Sensory Experience in the precise ways they desire and intend. In the real world, however, external influences often weaken one's sexiness flow, affecting factors such as the quality, quantity and even conceptualization of one's experience. High intention to exude or experience sensual pleasure could be muted by weak signal flow; for example, an individual may perceive him or herself as having high sexual prowess but experience a bodily injury that imposes new limits on what they could once accomplish or affects their sexual self-esteem. Conversely, feedback occurs when external factors are too high in intensity, distorting sexiness output. An example of this may be a case of an individual experiencing fetishization by lovers who only visualize them through the lens of Black sexual stereotypes, overriding the volume of their own authentic sexual expression.

One final note about External Influences and sexiness engineering in general: in an ideal engineering scenario, an individual is in full charge of their control panel, maintaining good gain levels and moving their sliders in a manner that is comfortable or authentic to them. If they do not have full control—as in the case of a child or someone with limited self-mastery—they are in the care of someone who is actively working to help the individual grow in their capacity to self-cultivate their sexiness. In nonoptimal cases, an individual may experience involuntary or forced slider movement or gain that is too weak or overpowering. In any case, however, and at any given moment, an individual's sexiness control panel exists as a constelled web of sliders, exhibiting a cumulative expression of exuded being and sensory experience.

And What Of Race?

Reiterating the premise of this book, it is important to remind you, the reader, that Black Sexual Epistemology is a model theorizing about *racialized* sexuality, which is to say that race is an included aspect therein. The specialized focus on African Americans in this study was driven by my particular desire to uncover potential ways that African Americans might be influenced in their sexual social construction by the particular history of sexualized racism and anti-Blackness in the United States. There is no question, in looking at the data, that race has influenced the ways African Americans in this sample think about sexuality and their sexual selves. There are two specific ways that race appears in this model: through the Performative Blackness channel of sexiness and as an adverse External Influence.

When asked the two specific questions related to this notion, most participants had no shortage of examples of how race, and specifically racism, maligned their exuded being and quality of sensory experience. Responses to the race question were so commonly negative that I eventually had to add an additional question asking if participants could identify positive effects of race along with the negative.[2] Despite this emphasis, reports of negative effects were limited in scope to participants' perceived inability to access or effectively cultivate sexiness aspects and not necessarily how sexiness itself was conceptualized. Stated more plainly, being Black did not seem to negatively affect participants' understanding of what sexiness was more than it affected their perceived ability to be or access sexiness in the ways they most desired.

Participants did not mention anti-Blackness by name, nor speak on any of its related concepts until the specific question of "being Black" was asked. Though slightly fewer in number, those who mentioned elements of Blackness ahead of the specific questions about race referred to it positively when identifying perceived aspects of sexiness—for example, "skin tone," "African American women," "natural hair." In light of this, I've determined that while anti-Blackness is a significant modifier of African Americans' relationship with sexiness and sexuality, it is most salient in this model as an "External Influence," positionally on par with other themes mentioned by respondents in the study, which will be discussed further in Chapter 6. Racial elements offered for the sexiness question appear qualitatively different in the data and thus have their own category, "Performative Blackness," within the conceptual theme of Exuded Being.

I want to insert one additional story into this section of the book that reifies the salient yet potentially insidious nature of racialization and race consciousness when it comes to sexuality. It is a retelling of an experience that happened early on in my data collection process while speaking with Mary, a cisgender Philadelphia woman in her mid-30s. When I originally asked about the influence of race on her sex life, Mary reported that there was none. This was no problem to me, as the point of asking the question was to make sure I made no assumptions about what race and racialization have meant to my target population. That said, in her post-interview reflection Mary almost reflexively invited race back into the room by informing me that she was preparing to get married and was currently working on improving her fellatio technique because, as she put it, "my fiancé's been with white girls." The cognitive mechanisms involved in Mary's oversight are beyond the scope of this theory; however, that this happened raises important implications that will be addressed toward the end of this book.

Chapter Summary

To reiterate, then, Black Sexual Epistemology describes an ideology that begins within the mind of a sexual engineer, or Erotic Self. Erotic selves participate in intentional activities that produce Sexiness—a personal soundscape of sexual frequencies made up of Exuded Being or Sensory Experience. The production of sexiness, while not always achieved, is almost always intended, as its development aids in the individual's sense of fulfillment and self-mastery. This process of sexual cultivation and expression is fulfilled through eight specific channels: Comportment, Corporeality, Erotic Energy, Performative Blackness, Sensual Pleasure, Relationship, Mental Excitation and Positive Affect. The development process is, at times, moderated by "external influences" (including but not limited to anti-Blackness). Collectively, the interaction of these elements within an individual in conjunction with the interactions engaged in by other erotic beings ultimately works to establish the erotic universe that is Sexuality. The next chapter extends further into the BSE model by exploring the particular components of Exuded Being.

Notes

1 Robbins, S., Chatterjee, P., & Canda, E. (2006). *Contemporary human behavior theory: A critical perspective for social work* (2nd ed.). Boston, MA: Allyn and Bacon.
2 To this latter question, one participant did not feel she could identify positive effects of any kind related to being a Black sexual being.

References

Robbins, S., Chatterjee, P., & Canda, E. (2006). *Contemporary human behavior theory: A critical perspective for social work* (2nd ed.). Boston, MA: Allyn and Bacon.

3

EXUDED BEING

MONICA AND RAMSEY'S STORY

Monica (biracial, age 33) and Ramsey (dark-skinned, age 37) are a couple living in Atlanta, Georgia; they have been married for seven years. They met in their early 20s after Ramsey coached Monica's son in a youth basketball league. At the time they met, Monica had only had one other sexual partner (her son's father); Ramsey, by contrast, had had many previous partners, including another young woman with whom he had a child at 21. Monica grew up with two white parents in a predominantly white, religiously conservative community in Kentucky. She moved to Atlanta for college after graduating from high school and quickly became more immersed in African American cultural experiences there. Her unexpected pregnancy at 19 proved to be a big disappointment to her community back home, and while her family did not disown her, they did pass significant judgment on Monica for not waiting until she was married or at least out of college to have a baby. (Note: it did not help that the child's father was Black and chose not to stay in Monica's life.) Many of Ramsey's previous partners had been friends from high school who were sex workers—women who either danced for money at local clubs or performed sexual acts for money through alternate venues. While Ramsey had no problem having sex with any of his previous partners, he says he ultimately chose to pursue a more serious relationship with Monica because, in his eyes, "she's a good girl, and while those girls were cool, they weren't the type anybody would want to settle down with."

After seven years of marriage Ramsey and Monica are now at a crossroads, as the pressures of parenting and married life have started to take a toll on their sex life. For Monica, the question of whether she settled down too soon lingers along with the fear that she is not getting all the pleasure she could get from her sex life. At times she has considered leaving Ramsey but chooses not to out of regret for the previous disappointment she caused her family and for the ways her marriage has allowed her to present some sense of rectification for her previous "mistakes." For Ramsey, married life still provides the #RelationshipGoals he's always wanted; however, it leaves much to be desired, as while he enjoys the emotional connection he's made with Monica, he has found sex with her to be not as interesting as the sex he used to have. (Note: within the most recent three years of their marriage, Ramsey resumed a secret side relationship with a sex worker he'd known prior to meeting Monica and still visits with her on a quarterly basis.)

All erotic beings, by virtue of their am-ness, are capable of expressing sexiness. To fulfill that aim, however, they must exude in a way that is effectively perceived, whether by one's own or another Erotic Self. This chapter delves further into the concept of Exuded Being, or the dimensions and characteristics of sexiness that are literally "exuded," or given off, energetically by an erotic being. Exudation is in the eye of those attracted to it, which means an individual may be perceived as exuding "organic" sexiness without actively trying or be deemed as being more "authentically" sexy because they don't attempt or wish to exude it. Exuded being can be intentional, unintentional or, as is more likely the case, a mixture of the two.

From a BSE perspective, sexiness lives and is present in an erotic being long before one ever becomes an Erotic Self; however, lack of awareness of one's sexiness can prevent an erotic being from recognizing or exuding it in any discernable way. Moreover, low exudation from any erotic being may preclude another individual's ability to witness, or "hear," their sexiness, thus stunting one's sexiness development process. A person may incorporate supports that enhance personal exudation volume, such as adorning certain clothing or other personal effects or engaging in activities that trigger sensory or energetic shifts (e.g., engaging in yoga or listening to uplifting music/reciting affirmations to increase confidence and self-esteem). Deliberately attempting to raise one's exudation volume does not disqualify an individual from accessing sexiness. Moreover, without outside influence individuals may concern themselves with optimizing volume for their own personal enjoyment—exuding as a means to trigger their own sensory experiences—long before they interact with another erotic being.

Although Exuded Being extends most readily from human beings, it does not end there and can be attributed to both animate and inanimate objects (e.g., "food," "fantasies") and nonhuman living entities (e.g., "nature"). There are four main channels through which a person may engineer exuded being; their names and dimensions follow.

Comportment

Comportment is, in many ways, a central element of exuded being. Briefly, it refers to one's behavior or way of moving in the world ("mannerisms," "how they carry themselves"). A person may present as reserved and subdued or outgoing and jovial, with both temperaments having the potential to attract others to them. In this way, individuals determine the extent of their willingness/ability to interact with other erotic beings based on their perceptions of that being's comportment. According to respondents, Comportment is indicative of how one shows up in the world, establishing it as the strongest, most popular baseline for engendering attraction between erotic beings. Carlton, a Midwest man in his early 20s, shared this perspective: "[i]t's not more of how you look than of who you are that attracts me sexually . . . because you can be the cutest person in the world, but your attitude is just shit. It's just horrible." From another area of the country, Carmen, who is in her early 40s, offered a similar argument: "[y]ou may not be necessarily attractive to me in more of a physical type of way. But you could have a great personality, and that's a sexy thing." In this way, comportment is not only essential to the center of exuded being; it may also have the capacity to override perceived deficits in other sexiness channels.

There were four emergent types of comportment deemed to be sexiness by the research sample: *confidence, compassion, competence* and *self-sovereignty*. While all erotic beings have some type of comportment, it was established that true exuded being reflects the best of these particular comportment types. For most respondents, *confidence* was the single most popular term used to exemplify this channel, perceived as a necessary sexiness trait for both others and the self. Related terms included *self-possession, assertiveness, self-esteem, pride, ambition* and *being bold*. While an erotic being's own sense of confidence need not be high to witness it in others, respondents were clear that personal confidence was essential to high exudation volume.

Confidence can be clothed in a variety of different attire, languages, etc., yet it is assumed to be most clearly present when it is poised, self-assured and, at minimum, gives the impression that the individual is fully comfortable in one's own body and mind. Jasmine, a 20-something in Philadelphia explained that "when you're secure in yourself and you know yourself as well as possible, you're able to be sexy." Fiasco, a queer, gender non-binary person in Washington, D.C., offered more detail:

> I think sexiness is in tandem, or a form of confidence? But I wanted to be explicit about what kind of confidence; it's about owning our energy . . . when you're able to own and harness that energy [so that] essentially you can turn anything about yourself into sexiness, down to, you know, how you put your socks on.

Fiasco's explanation makes a link between Comportment and another channel, Erotic Energy, in that while both are sexiness in and of themselves, an individual may perceive someone as having a greater exudation volume of the former because of how well the latter is controlled. Ava, a heterosexual Philadelphia woman in her mid-20s, referred to this when she discussed sexiness as someone being "calm." Specifically, she stated that

> if you're, like, not braggy or arrogant about, like, the greatness that you are, whether it be, like, physical attractiveness or, like, sexually good in bed, like *that* attracts me. It's like you calm with it, you like, 'You gon' see. You gon' find out.' I like that.

In this example, high erotic energy volume combined with balanced, mid-range confidence volume signaled increased attractiveness by the observer.

"Compassion," "openness" and "humility" were all additional traits participants reported as other forms of exuded comportment. While confidence led the list, most participants were clear that this trait should be matched with a sense of *compassion* for others and willingness to be inclusive in how one's confidence was shared. As 40-year-old Darius noted, for example, "I can assert myself and my opinions and my thoughts and stuff without belittling somebody else. The balance of knowing how to do that? *That's sexy*." Jewel identified "consideration" as a form of compassion showing up in the bedroom during coital activity: "[d]o they consider me? Are they considering the way my body rises and falls and the noises that I'm making, the connection that we're having and the environment . . ." For Jasmine in New York, compassion took on a more global scope, with them favoring it from others in the form of making tangible commitments to social justice ideals:

> [i]f someone is like, "Yeah, I, you know . . . yes, I agree with the things Martin Luther King said, but I don't think that we should close Rikers [Island Penitentiary]," that's not sexy to me. Like, where, where is the thought in that? That doesn't make any sense; it doesn't go any further than that.

Exuding confidence is a perceived strength, often implying the ability to comfort, support, protect/defend, physically satisfy and, in some cases, positively influence or inspire others, including those who may not feel the same perceived level of confidence in themselves. These abilities may also be considered forms of *competence*, another strongly heralded aspect of comportment reported by the sample. Examples of competence among the sample ranged widely and included "being smart and in control," "good grooming," "street savvy," "knowing your body in every way possible" and "having a sense of style." Mary in Philadelphia referred to this quality symbolically with general regard to relationships: "I'm not attracted to fixer-uppers, like oh my God, you have to get them together because they're 35 and still with their mom or they're 50 years old and renting a room, like oh my gosh . . ." Qui, a pansexual woman in North Carolina, referred to forms of competence called upon in sexual negotiation:

> knowing that you can communicate your boundaries. Knowing that when you do feel wronged, you know how to go about correcting it.

Whether it means letting that person know, like, "Hey, this is how you crossed my boundaries; I don't appreciate it. Um, you know, if we can't come to some kind of consensus, then I'll be forced to leave you alone." You know, something like that.

In both Mary and Qui's examples, the individual in question exudes behaviors that are perceived to exist within the range of "incapable" and "highly capable" in the area deemed of particular importance by the observer: life skills for Mary and sexual negotiation for Qui. Coming across individuals with competence volume drew each woman in for the potential sensory experience and could have served as a sensory experience in and of itself. While verbal and nonverbal forms of confidence can give an observer the impression that they are interacting with a competent exuded being, being able to witness the individual's competence in action may add weight to the observer's initial impressions, providing more tangible evidence of genuinely high exudation.

If confidence and competence represent the being and doing of comportment, *self-sovereignty* may represent the spirit underlying them both. The ability to resist conventional thinking or resist the desire to hold back one's self is the essential quality of self-sovereignty, reported most notably as "freedom," "feeling free at all times," "authentic," "unapologetic," "independent" and "openness." As some respondents noted, owning one's sexuality requires a certain sense of freedom that transcends traditional rules about how one must act or behave. These traditions often inspire fear and hesitation among individuals, which is why they are particularly attractive when resisted. Lola evoked the notion of self-sovereignty when speaking about her wardrobe: "I have a big chest [*giggles*]. So I like to show it off, and so, when I have the freedom to wear what I want to wear, like, it makes me feel good." King in Columbus, Ohio, described their autonomy as being "very attracted to people who are free-spirited . . . who are just open minded to, you know, everything and everyone. I'm a very open person. I just kinda go with the flow, and I've always just been free." Saucy Teal described the relationship even more succinctly: "[u]ltimately, sexiness is liberation of thyself. And sexiness can look like this person, who could be a secretary or librarian or whoever—um, teacher, what have you."

In summary, the cumulative quality of Comportment refers to an individual who is aware of and able to comfortably assert one's sense of self, needs and desires. They are self-possessed and able to take care of themselves, their own and others' needs without becoming codependent. They are obviously unaffected by a need to fit convention while showing genuine mindfulness and consideration for others. Finally, an individual with high comportment is actively open to the organic, authentic ways that opportunities for growth and connection show up in their lives.

Corporeality

Every erotic being possesses a container in which their sexiness is housed. For some in this sample, the presence and particularities of this container are themselves a source of exudation. I refer to this as Corporeality—regarding the nature and elements of the physical body or that which is material or tangible. Sexiness, according to the sample, exudes from bodies that have clearly prominent or "high" corporeal volume, including "natural hair"; "clear, smooth skin"; "full lips"; and "large breasts," buttocks, "thighs" and genitals. As Magenta, a cisgender, heterosexual woman in Washington, D.C., noted, "Just in general, you know, a person that has, like, extra assets to them, um, you know, it's pretty sexy to me." For most respondents, corporeality referred to the nature or presence of specific body parts; for others, the fact of a body's presence in and of itself was sufficient. In the cases of Magenta and Rocky, observations and assessment of corporeal volume ran concurrent with their own body ownership/affirmation process:

> I put "curves" because, I don't know, like, I've always thought that I was beautiful. Um, I still think that I am beautiful, and the more that I'm seeing how the media is now catching on to the beauty behind curvy women, it's like, I been there, done that.
>
> (Magenta)

> Rocky: Well, I have a body . . . and . . . uh, there are some parts of my body that I think are sexy, and there are some parts of my body that I don't think are sexy. And it is an ongoing relationship—like, I'm currently right now, in my life, really focused on improving my relationship with my body; hence, I even just got some [tattoo] work done yesterday . . . that's one of the ways I am claiming

	ownership of my body and, like, driving my relationship with my body . . .
Me:	Okay. And so are tattoos—your own tattoos—a source of sexiness for you?
Rocky:	Yes, I think I'm sexy with my tattoos [*laughs*]. I think my tattoos are sexy.

In the same way as with Comportment, both examples highlight the ability of individuals to consider, cultivate and bear witness to their own corporeal exudation, sometimes when inspired by or brought into relationship with other erotic beings.

Bodies were not the only entities deemed corporeally significant to respondents in the sample. To a smaller degree some inanimate objects, including cars, shoes, clothing and body adornments (e.g., "belts" or "tattoos," as noted earlier), reified the salience of corporeality as a construct. Inanimate objects can enhance the corporeal exudation of the body they are connected to, as 20-something queer femme Luna noted:

> I will see a person and not be that interested, and then I'll see a picture of them with glasses and be like, "*Oh, Hello.*" And I'm suddenly way more attracted, and . . . I don't even know what that is; I don't know where it came from.

Objects can also be employed in amplifying one's own corporeal volume, as married 30-something-year-old Leslie observed on the night of her bachelorette party: "someone gifted me this dress . . . and I just remember feeling—I had my makeup done, and I just remember this as the last time I remember just feeling like I was super sexy!" Inanimate objects may also possess their own exudation volume while serving as stand-ins for human bodies or body parts. Fifty-year-old Philadelphian Taquaan discussed as much in his assessment of a popular sports car:

> The Corvette is the number one selling, um, sports car in the United States in the past, like, 40 years. And it's always had pretty much the same body style. Um, and the Corvette has been the only car that has consistently, in 40 or 50 years, been shaped like a woman. . . . When people say, "What a nice car!" and I'm thinking to myself, "Has anyone ever thought that that's actually shaped just like a woman?" . . . I'm attracted to curves.

It is interesting to note that femme and femininity-assigned erotic beings were disproportionately identified by all genders as examples of corporeal exudation. I will discuss femininity as sexiness later on in the chapter; however, it is significant to acknowledge its place here, particularly in the common establishment of "curves" as a corporeal sexiness marker.

Performative Blackness

While many respondents' experiences of sex and race were problem-based, there was still sexiness perceived by some in the Performative Blackness of other Black people and Black culture in general. *Performative Blackness* as a BSE term comes directly from "quare" studies pioneer E. Patrick Johnson (2003), who coined the notion as a way to articulate how "Blackness" and its by-products have both served and potentially hampered African American communities. Johnson's premise is that Blackness, embodied by African American social expression (e.g., language, speech patterns, dress), is essentially nebulous, consisting of being or becoming that shifts according to the personal or political agenda of those expressing it. This shifting, he suggests, is most often determined by—and, by extension, constitutive of—the consistent discursive exchange between various subsets of African American people (in this case) looking to validate their own self-perception and worldview. This idea is particularly significant, in that it helps explain certain psychological aspects of African Americans' larger resistance to U.S. White supremacist ideology. As it relates to sexuality, performativity serves, in theory, as an intermediary between African Americans and sexualized racism by helping them establish lived parameters for true, "authentic" Black sexuality that resists the overarching pathological narrative. Elizabeth in Washington, D.C., opined that

> I think in so many ways, it feels very empowering to me—you know, my Blackness and my sexual identity and my sex*iness*, I guess . . . when I thought about Blackness and *my* Blackness and, um, how it related to my sexiness, it just felt like this inherent kinda thing now—like, Blackness *is sexy*.

Citing historical links between artistic expressions of the past and present (e.g., indigenous tribal dancing vs. twerking), elements of Black language and vernacular (e.g., rap music lyrics), participants identified a continuous beauty and attractiveness within Black culture along with a perceived intrinsic sexual ethos that permeated throughout. Alex, a 60-plus-year-old gay man living in New York, shared more of these sentiments:

> [w]hen I think about Blackness and how sexuality manifests itself through the Black experience, automatically the thing that comes to my mind is music. It's the way we dance. It's the way we dress. It's the way we move. It's the way we walk. I think we express our sexuality in the way we walk. Uh, we express our sexuality—crazy enough as it sounds—in the food, in the meals we prepare. You know, "I'm doing this for my *man* . . ." You know? . . . it comes out, and that's why I love, because for me, the Black experience, that's how I see our sexuality. And that's something that we have always—I feel—we innately have. And a lot of people may not automatically connect it with sex, but I've always thought about it that way. You know, that sensual kinda thing—that's very sexy . . . that's how I feel. Sexiness manifests itself through Black experience.

Encapsulating the point in a final sentiment, Elizabeth affirmed:

> [t]here's a boldness, um, to [Black culture] and, like, the raw quality of that that's really intriguing to me and speaks to, um, speaks to the ways that we see each other, speaks to the way we interact with each other as humans, and, um, a lot of that has to do with sex, frankly. A lot of that does come back to sex and sexiness.

While many respondents' affinity for Blackness was aesthetic (e.g., "natural hair," "dark skin," "big lips"), several respondents remarked about the personal quality of Black comportment,[1] most commonly sharing the off-handed assertion "ain't nothing like a Black man." *Swagger* was another term referred to by several of the respondents, speaking to a perception of uniquely cool comportment exhibited in the presentation of Black, predominantly male-identified, bodies. Ashley in North Carolina noted that she would never refuse a relationship with a man from another race if she were attracted to him, but her ultimate aspirations were clear: "[y]eah, I wanna [marry a Black man]. I wanna have Black kids and . . . be for the culture . . ." Betty, a 30-something woman in Kentucky, expressed some of the most explicit statements about Blackness as a relationship preference, putting the word *Blackness* in bold and centered on her initial primer sheet:

> I wrote "Blackness" because that's where it starts for me. . . . I have never been in a relationship with anybody other than—well, with anybody who identifies with anything other than Black. I haven't actually had the opportunity to. And when I was younger I wanted to date a white guy, and I wanted to date an Italian guy because that was what I saw on TV. I felt like Black men didn't want me because I looked so different . . . [but then] I hit 30 and was like, "There's no way [*laughs*]." Becoming more aware how Blackness is treated in America and how down I have been for Black men my entire life, I'm like, "There is *no* way."

Performative Blackness serves as a sexiness attraction point for the ways that Black people are believed to exhibit culturally specific exuded being. As Betty also hinted, the racialized experience of being Black creates an additional touch point in which some respondents feel automatic intimacy and emotional affinity with erotic others. As she went on to share, "Black is just so rich to me with history and experience, I just don't feel like another race would get it."

While Black men appeared to receive the bulk of cultural praise among respondents, they were not alone. Astro, a heterosexual Philadelphia man in his early 50s, extolled the particular virtues of "thick," "dark-skinned" Black women from all walks of life, including his mother and other women who'd raised him. As he reflected,

> African American women are just sexy *by definition* . . . in general, I think Black women are confident, strong . . . knowing who they are . . . they can come into an atmosphere and don't get swallowed up by anybody.

This quality of being able to hold one's own is both comportment and competence yet merging again with culturally specific perceptions about the simultaneous performance of race and gender for Black women. It is this latter point as well as the larger comprehensive points about Black cultural expression that separates Performative Blackness conceptually from other channels.

It's important to reiterate the resistive aspects of Performative Blackness that constitute how it's often used. While the challenges of racialization have been plenty, some African Americans find themselves leaning into

Performative Blackness as a means to reclaim the parts of themselves lost through racialization's anti-Black aspects. Jewel, a 30-something queer femme in Atlanta, raised this point while speaking about her aesthetic preferences in dating partners:

> [t]all and curvy are what I like, but I also think that is a part of this radicalization that continues to happen as I get older, which is that it's not what society . . . says [sexiness is] to be . . . that reverberates in my life, in the sense of the deprogramming of myself in really being an actor in White supremacy and anti-Blackness . . .

Leslie offered a similar sentiment when thinking of her own sexiness:

> I think someone can be sexy without being conventionally attractive.[2] I think that's also important, too, especially as someone who is not considered conventionally attractive by, like, European beauty standards. . . . I can still be sexy [*laughs*], you know? Even if there are people who may not think that I'm pretty.

In both cases the women appeared well aware of the expectations presented by mainstream society to reject Black femininity and Black beauty, choosing instead to value them anyway. And in their own way this particular act of resistance—choosing one's self when there is no external incentive to do so—serves as a source and mechanism of sexiness development in and of itself.

Erotic Energy

In Chapter 2 I introduced Sexiness as being an attractive energy linked to an individual's personal pleasure or fulfillment. For some respondents within the sample, the presence of this energy itself is considered sexiness—long before its expressive qualities occur. There is at least some sense that this energy is spiritual in nature. In any case, *Erotic Energy* is the term I use here to name it, referring to a physiological quality that, as one respondent put it, "*sets off* feelings of sexual or physical attraction and/or arousal" (italics mine). This was not a commonly named quality of sexiness, which is why it has its own separated channel from the others. That said, Erotic Energy was described as being so raw and fundamental to sexiness among those who mentioned it that in many ways it could arguably serve as ground zero for all other channels of Exuded Being, if not the BSE model as a whole. Indeed, if Comportment, Corporeality and Performative Blackness reflect what shows up on the outside of an erotic being, then Erotic Energy may be the primary frequency (or "carrying") impelling each signal to exist. As Fiasco in Washington, D.C., put it, "[Y]ou have stimulation, which is like 'Ooh!'—what makes you tingle . . . the erotic is *why* it makes you tingle . . ." Several respondents referred to Erotic Energy explicitly as "the erotic"; other terms included *aura, energy, waves, life source* and *vibe*.

Of all the channels, Erotic Energy is perhaps the most difficult to conceptualize, as its inherent principle is that of palpable indefinability. That said, Erotic volume appeared to have, among respondents, five distinct elements: Attraction, Fluidity, Depth, Power and "The Unknowable." Attraction refers most clearly to the magnetic pull experienced by one Erotic Self toward another. As Denise, a 30-something heterosexual woman in Chicago, explained it,

> [An erotic being] may not be giving it to you, it could just be you projecting or creating this ideal of a person, but, like, you're attracted to what's in front of you and it's . . . sometimes it's just very plain. Like, it's just . . . it's kinda inexplicable.

For some respondents, attraction is not automatic and is only made real or sustained through conversation or other cultivation process. From other perspectives, attraction is a much more raw sensation, coming about with little to no prompting. For Dana, a bisexual 40-plus-year-old in Detroit, true attraction is not cultivated at all but exists naturally, without provocation:

> [f]or you to *really* find someone sexy? There's almost like that initial animal attraction that you have. . . . I just feel like, on a real organic level, people either are sexy or they're not, for real. And it's okay if you're not sexy, but it just is or isn't there.

Attraction on the part of at least one Erotic Self can lead to arousal or desire—largely sexual in nature, though not necessarily so. During our conversation, Denise went on to describe desire as a "craving . . . not always craving that person in particular, but craving things about that person you admire." Taquaan, introduced earlier in the chapter through his perspective on vehicles, described attraction as leading to, for him, a "comfortable arousal . . ." not led by the genitals but still physiological and persistently evocative—not occurring solely as part of a sexual encounter.

Fluidity most strongly refers to an organic, unorganized, unbound energetic flow between Erotic Selves. It can occur in a sexual encounter in which all parties negotiate their way through random sensual activities—"just seduction, just kissing, just . . ." as Victoria in Buffalo described it—or it can vary in the source or mode of transmission, as Fiasco noted: "for some folks, their erotic is in what they see, and for some folks their erotic is in what they feel—but more so like the actual sensation of touch [or] what they hear." Several participants noted experiencing Erotic Energy as subtle or flowing, speaking particularly about the particular type of energy they find themselves attracted to. When Leola, a heterosexual North Carolina woman in her mid-20s, first began her interview with me, she drew across the primer sheet she was given a series of waves and swirls in various shades of blue and green marker, which appeared similar to an ocean floor. When I asked her what her images meant, she likened them to an ideal sexiness in which

> two individuals—or anyone—can just, I guess, flow with each other. . . . [S]ometimes when playing off those vibes you just get the extra "oomph" . . . it's just the act and just how you're flowing through the day. . . . I am walking in my own space and whoever sees me sees me, and if not, I don't care!

Though her emphasis was on the flow of said expression, Leola's description of her own sexiness expression feels reminiscent of both confidence and self-sovereignty, speaking again to the relationship between Erotic Energy and other channels.

Combining fluidity with attraction, one can also experience shifting attractions among various sexes and genders as a function of Erotic Energy. During my conversation with 20-something college student Keishawna, she noted,

> I identify as straight, but I could see a woman and I could be like, "That's a sexy woman," and not wanna sleep with that woman, but, like, she's alluring to me. Or, like a guy, vice versa—it's like, they're alluring to me.

Central to combining these elements is not just the shifting of attraction but also the allowing of space for said organic shifts to occur, without outside force, provocation or limitation.

That Erotic Energy is fluid should not discount its capacity for depth, as it can and often does possess this quality as well. Depth refers to aspects of the erotic that are not readily apparent on the surface of an attractive individual or sexual encounter. To respondents, these are "qualities that go beyond just 'being pretty'"; "so much more than what's on the physical"; or "the natural vibe that I know that's inside of you, deep down." Deep aspects of erotic energy include but are not limited to an individual's authentic personal thoughts, secret philosophies, private insecurities, hidden emotions or unspoken spiritual beliefs. In some ways depth can be an aspect of other channels as well, as several respondents pointed to it as a necessary part of their sensory experience. For example, Samantha, a cisgender heterosexual woman in Delaware, cited erotic depth as a primary requirement for sexual fulfillment:

> [s]ex is like, we're sitting down and I have to be willing to become you. That's how I look at it, literally. Yeah, it's that deep. We're joining as one; like, I have to be willing to become you. So I have to trust you in here [*motions to abdominal area*] and trust [myself] enough to trust me over there and us being one and what we're creating. I mean, that's a crazy amount of trust.

Though it remains an exudation within the BSE model, Samantha's example could add a second dimension, such that depth can potentially be seen in two different ways—as simultaneously "being deep" and "going deep."

Witnessing deep erotic exudation generally requires atypical individual effort and is thus assumed to be more valuable when it is accessed. As Jewel, a queer woman in her 30s, stated,

> I feel like so many people . . . live on the surface of life . . . just checking shit off and doing whatever; they don't ever really figure out why they're struggling with things and really get in the dirt and minutiae of life. So those type [sic] of people attract me, like people who have really changed themselves and, like, really worked hard to become better.

It is both the perceived scarcity and assumed authenticity involved in revealing one's depth that increase its value and some respondents' desire to access it.

In the same way that it is fluid, attractive and deep, Erotic Energy is also powerful, capable of endowing its possessor with increased power over themselves and others. In the BSE model, erotic *power* speaks to the capacity some individuals have to negotiate influence over themselves and other erotic beings—most often through sensory experience. For some, like Taquaan, power comes through the exertion of control: "[being] in positions of power, in positions of control . . . [exerting] strength, but not strength in muscle . . . decision-making, leadership . . ." For others, like Lisa in Buffalo, power comes through the exact opposite action, or the relinquishing of control: "in giving away my control, I have it because he's doing exactly what I want him to do." Velvet Lips, a queer Atlanta femme in her late 30s, offered a foundational way to think about how power operates here:

> [t]he elements of power consist of the agency to display with your body . . . how you look at people, the way you move and how, uh, you use that agency to, um, show your confidence and your power . . .

She went on to specifically cite seduction as the active function of power, explaining it as

> your ability to use your agency to seduce people and to influence people in the way that you want. . . . I think that seduction plays a role because that sexiness can be used not only for lovers or partners but for coworkers, for, you know, platonic friendships . . . yes, it can play a role within sexuality in who *you* are attracted to and who *you personally* can influence, but I think that in a broader sense, sexiness and seduction can, overall, play out in your life in much different ways.

Much erotic power appears to exist in sexual spaces—and often between lovers; however, as both Taquaan and Velvet noted, it is not limited to such spaces and does not require coital activity, or even coital intentions, to be present. For Jade in Philadelphia, this sentiment is echoed by the ability to exert influence over one's own erotic self:

> if I'm working out, if I'm lifting something very strong I feel sexy. But it's not physically I wouldn't be, I don't feel physically like, attractively sexy

because I'm sweaty and I'm gross and stuff? But inwardly I feel that sense of "AAARGGGGH! I can do this!" or "I'm empowered!"

Ultimately, any context in which an individual utilizes one's ability to influence or be influenced by others may also indicate an exertion of erotic power.

Despite my best attempts to describe Erotic Energy here, there is still an unavoidable sense of ambiguity that makes up part of its core nature. Because of its inability to be fully defined, I've labeled this last quality *The Unknown*. As noted by members of the sample, The Unknown is an "understanding beyond words"—that which is known on an intuitive level, and even felt to a certain degree physiologically, but which most individuals lack the ability to fully articulate or discuss. Several respondents expressed this challenge of not being able to articulate what they knew in this regard. In Rockville, Maryland, Leslie remarked, "Like . . . you know, it's like a feeling. You can *feel* sexy . . . it's really hard for me to explain." George, a transgender Brooklyn, New York, man in his late 20s, noted, "I know when something turns me on, but I don't necessarily know if something is sexy to me if it turns me on. . . . I don't really have a good grasp on that." While some of this limited awareness may represent a lack of previous consideration of the subject, or even true unknowability (aspects that are forever inaccessible to the human mind), the fact that it is still "known" by some individuals may speak to a larger dynamic: being limited by constraints of the English language and even—to a certain extent—American or other Western (read Eurocentric) ways of knowing.

Aaron, an "Other"-identified individual who is in their late 30s and living in Philadelphia, was one of the first people I interviewed for this study and one of the first to speak intently about the "label-less-ness" of Erotic Energy. While they were able to draw some physical representations of sexiness (eyes, face) on their initial primer sheet, they acknowledged upon explanation that the images were "more concrete than I would define." Going on to speak about both depth and intensity, Aaron acknowledged that for them, true sexiness exists in a space that is unbounded by gender, sexual orientation or labels in general. A small number of other respondents referred to the erotic as being explicitly masculine or feminine; however, Aaron raised an interesting counterpoint to this when they asserted, "I feel like it's a colonial leftover that we need to name everything." They provided the following historical reference for their claim:

> [y]ou know, just to . . . the idea of colonization sweeping across this country and changing the native imperatives which dealt with . . . being Two-Spirit, for example. They had a name for it, but it was just like it . . . [it was] only because they had such a sense of their spirituality, it was more housed in *that* than it was labeling. And, you know, putting people in areas based on labels and stuff, like that, it was just like, "Oh yeah. That, you know, that's what that means because the spirits have blessed you with, you know, this feeling here and this feeling here." And you're just, that's how you live, you know?

This perspective was consistent with that of other interviewees, who talked specifically about their own sense of gender divergence even while—in some cases—still identifying with the gender assignment they were given at birth. Fiasco, referenced earlier in this section, spoke to their experience of this divergence when they described Erotic Energy as

> a mish-mash . . . not just, you know, living in this pseudo-masculine or pseudo-feminine "that's all I am, there's nothing else" type of energy . . . all of these things are in me, and I can harness them in any form as [sic] I choose.

From this perspective, it is possible that in the push to name and find consensus on particular experiences of gender and sexuality, the ability to speak fully about the fluidity of Erotic Energy may have potentially gotten lost in translation to English from indigenous language counterparts—not just in what would become the United States but also in other areas in the world.

This marks the end of concepts related specifically to the four channels of Sexiness constitutive of Exuded Being: Comportment, Corporeality, Performative Blackness and Erotic Energy. I continue in Chapter 4 with the four channels of Sensory Experience: Sensual Pleasure, Mental Excitation, Relationship and Positive Affect.

Notes

1. There is evidence to suggest that Black cultural expression has unique temporal and geographic links to the continent, from African Americans and others in the diaspora in the present day. The way that Blackness as sexiness was described among the sample is reminiscent of Black "cool," a description of Afro-descended culture and aesthetic that emphasizes control, composure and the ability to master one's ceremony. Robert Farris Thompson is considered the premier scholar on this topic, having studied its origins on various parts of the Continent and its connection to contemporary African American art forms, including music, fashion and visual art. Black cool is not limited, however, to a description of art; it is an ideological practice that pervades even the most common activities of many communities.
2. The term *conventionally attractive* and how Leslie refers to it here brings to mind the actress Viola Davis, who shared similar sentiments after being labeled "less classically beautiful" in a 2014 *New York Times* article: "I've heard that statement my entire life. Being a dark-skinned black woman—you hear it from the time you get out of the womb. Classically not beautiful is a fancy term of [sic] saying ugly and denouncing you, erasing you. Now it worked when I was younger; it no longer works for me now. . . . Because really at the end of the day, you define you."

Reference

Johnson, E. P. (2003). *Appropriating blackness: Performance and the politics of authenticity*. Durham, NC: Duke University Press.

4

SENSORY EXPERIENCE

TRAVIS'S STORY

Travis is a 28-year-old single gay man living in Portland, Oregon. He moved to Portland after graduating from the state university in his hometown and securing a lucrative corporate job with a tech company in the area. Travis was born and raised in Racine, Wisconsin, the older of two boys to a single mother. The last time Travis saw his father was at the age of three, shortly before he was arrested and sentenced to 30 years in federal prison on weapons possession, aggravated assault and drug trafficking charges. Travis's mother never remarried, often relying on Travis and his brother for male socioemotional support instead of pursuing another adult partner. While Travis did have other male support in his family at large, he often still felt like the "man of the house" and as if taking care of his mother and brother was his responsibility. When Travis was 14, he was picked up and harassed by local police while walking home from the school bus stop. The officers stopped him in a case of mistaken identity; however, the experience significantly traumatized Travis, leaving behind a fear of being outside alone that remains to the present day.

DOI: 10.4324/9781003022183-4

Travis never felt completely the same as other boys in his school and neighborhood, eventually identifying as gay right around the same time as the police incident. It was not until Travis went to college that he developed friendships with other gay men, only a handful of whom were Black but were either "messy," as Travis called them, or still in the closet. When it came to dating, Travis found himself dating only white men, which often required him to play down some of the social things he enjoyed (e.g., dance, playing cards and dominos, R&B/hip hop music) or suppress more sensitive parts of himself in order to be accepted. In looking back on his experiences, Travis finds that he enjoyed his friendships with Black gay men because of how they were able to bond with each other over the common experience of being Black men. By contrast, Travis found it easier to date white gay men because they were more open to the option of dating and being romantic publicly, but he never felt comfortable discussing his experiences of racism, or even his life in general, with them.

Now that Travis has been living in Portland he has found a more diverse group of men to date; however, being in a predominantly white city adds to his frustration with finding other Black gay men to be with—particularly ones who enjoy dating other Black men as well. (Note: usually, he is limited to those he meets while out of town for business conferences.) By contrast, Travis has found himself even more popular among white gay men in his area, although more often than not this is based on their perceptions of him being more assertive sexually and willing to dominate in the bedroom than a desire to know him as a multilayered human being. While Travis considers himself to have a healthy sex life, what he desires more than anything is a romantic partner with whom he can begin to become more emotionally transparent, especially when it comes to sharing parts of his past. He's also hoping to one day have someone special to introduce to his mother and brother, whom he still visits and supports back in Racine.

Of all the reasons an individual may engage with sexuality, the pursuit of how it makes them feel may well be at the top of the list. Whether it's the feeling of gratitude gained from receiving an unexpected compliment, the emotional closeness of hugging a loved one, the satisfaction experienced after an intended orgasm or the therapeutic benefit of meditation, one could argue that before anything else, erotic beings desire first and foremost to *feel good*. In the BSE model, this sensational aspect of sexiness is called Sensory Experience; it refers to all the ways that individuals experience pleasure through and within the body—including the mind and emotions. The inclusion of the last two as sensory experiences departs from typically Eurocentric epistemologies that assert a dichotomy between the mind and body, often with a demonization of the latter (Brown Douglas, 1999; Descartes & Voss, 1989). In the BSE model this distinction is erased, as sensory experiences reported among this sample were overwhelmingly experienced as some combination of simultaneous cognition, emotion and physiology. In some cases, cognition worked to influence emotion and physiology, such as a thought triggering involuntary heart palpitations and enamored feelings. In others, physiology and emotion transcended the mind, with metacognition coming thereafter or not at all. Black Sexual Epistemology establishes that though they are not "body parts" per se, experiences of mind and emotions are salient enough aspects of sensate sexiness to include them within the construct overall.

Though they are considered channels within the model, it is important to acknowledge that Sensory Experiences do not operate the same way on a sexiness control panel as Exuded Being. While Exuded Being begins from the inside and extends out, Sensory Experience proceeds in the opposite direction, pulled from the outside in toward the Erotic Self. As an individual moves about in the world, they may experience unexpected increases in their sensory experience levels based on engagement in experiences they did not initiate. If an individual intentionally raises the dial on a Sensory Experience channel, however, it may raise their own experience of that channel yet likely not before increasing their openness to initiating it or experiencing it being initiated with them. This is another key difference highlighting the heightened power inherent to Exuded Being: while External Influences (to be discussed in Chapter 6) can affect both dimensions of sexiness, they can more readily affect one's access to Sensory Experiences, which are more likely to involve interactions with others and are thus less controllable.

Sensual Pleasure, Mental Excitation, Positive Affect and Relationship make up the four channels of Sensory Experience. Like Exuded Being, as previously noted, sensory experiences usually happen when an individual engages in encounters with at least one other erotic being; however, they can also happen alone (e.g., experiencing a wet dream). In many ways, Sensory Experience provides the feedback loop to Exuded Being, in that fulfillment of the former usually serves to validate or affirm fulfillment of the latter. Sensory Experience can be fulfilled by any individual who has assessed exudation in an erotic being; this is how an erotic being might produce a Sensory Experience for someone else without actually seeing themselves as an intention-driven Erotic Self. Descriptions and examples of the four channels of Sensory Experience are provided in the remainder of this chapter.

Sensual Pleasure

Sensual Pleasure is the most popular channel of sensory experience and refers to activities that exude sexiness to the five senses of the outer body—sight, sound, touch, taste and smell. These include activities like "vaginal sex," "oral sex," "penetration" and "orgasms," though they may also involve noncoital activities, such as "holding hands," "kisses on the neck," "textures," "a dress that complements my figure just right" or "the feel of clean sheets on the naked skin." Sexual intercourse and other traditionally labeled, multisensory sexual acts ("masturbation," "fellatio," "cunnilingus"), activities driven primarily by touch or skin-to-skin/skin-to-object contact, were the most commonly reported sensory experiences among this sample. For example, Lalah, a heterosexual woman in her early 60s, immediately thought of coital activity when answering her primer sheet on sexiness:

> you know, visual . . . auditory. . . . What comes to mind is [the song] "S&M" with Rihanna. When she says, "Sex in the air, I love the smell of it." . . . smell, touch, uh, taste!

By contrast, Kim Fon Toy, a gay man in his late 20s, invoked touch-driven multisensory experience when discussing a "cuddle date":

> I like cuddling. Um, and cuddling could look like different things in many capacity [sic]. It could look like me laying on your chest. It could look like me laying in your lap and you laying in my bed. It could look many different ways as long as we have that touch and that closeness . . . and so, essentially, what a cuddle date is, instead of going out you can opt to stay in, watch a movie, cook some food—maybe order some Chinese or some pizza—um, stay in the bed, listen to music, [smoke marijuana], put some herbals in it [laughs]. Hit a J, have a little incense going, set the mood or, you know, even—yeah, set the mood.

Although Lalah's and Kim's experiences differ in their incorporation of traditional sexual intercourse, both involve an intermingling of the senses in a way that optimizes the feeling of sexiness for them.

Aesthetics, a term used by some in the sample, speaks to visual stimuli that are appealing or attractive to the viewer in question. *Beauty, physical attractiveness, physical appeal* and *what appeals to the eyes* were several other terms and phrases used to describe this particular quality. One respondent, a Philadelphia woman in her early 20s, defined beauty as "something of aesthetic value for which we have no *better* words availed [sic] to us" (italics mine); to some degree, this definition likely speaks to a perceived superficiality when considering the concept. While many respondents relied on aesthetics as a source of sexiness, most were quick to discount the validity of their assertions, using statements like "I made a point of that *not* being at the top of my list" or qualifying their perspectives by establishing them as personal versus universal preference: "not like society's standard of beauty, but it's kinda like, what *you* perceive as beautiful." In fact, out of all the sensual pleasures named by respondents, aesthetics were the qualities most likely to be noted as "culturally defined and informed." Regardless, it is clear that people find sensual pleasure in people, places and objects that exude high aesthetic corporeality or represent particular aspects of physical beauty.

Regarding this topic, there does seem to be a cultural influence on perceptions of beauty among this sample, which helps to establish additional validity for thinking about the influence of race. Many respondents noted specific attractions to "women of color"; "dark, dark skin"; and skin that is "mostly black, sometimes brown, rarely white" along with "kinky hair," "natural hair," "thick[ness]," "fat," "voluptuous[ness]," "healthy," "firm," "husky" and "curvy"—physical attributes often indirectly associated with Black bodies.[1] Astro, who shared his thoughts about the Performative Blackness of African American women in Chapter 3, suggested during our conversation that the assignment of sexiness to these specific types of bodily attributes may, in fact, be unique to Black people:

> our definition, you know, you kind of, um . . . I wouldn't say "meaty," but, you know, when you find the definition of beauty in Vogue and what not, they have these anorexic women, and they're portraying some type of beauty and, you know, that's, that wasn't part of what my norm was. . . . Even today I don't find that very . . . you know, it

looks good, you know—they do well in their portrayal, but that's not beauty to me . . .

> Me: So do you feel like [an affinity for large, proportional body types] was unique to being African American?
>
> Astro: As I travel, you know, in the Army, and I like to go to different places, and I see the differences, you know, I *believe* it was unique for our culture. Not saying it wasn't in other cultures, speaking from my own experience.

Regardless of whether or not the attribution of sexiness to Black bodies is universal among all African American people, there is still clear evidence to support the salience of cultural influence on the general establishment of aesthetics as sensual pleasure.

Body aesthetics is a main, though not exclusive, source of visual sensual pleasure for this group; the presence of color, for example, can be seen as having highly pleasurable sensory volume as well. Colors like oranges, purples, blues and greens can conjure up particular physiological sensations when they are encountered or can represent ideas (e.g., "warmth") that help the observer more readily access pleasure-based fantasies and desires. Camille, a Buffalo woman in her early 30s, spoke of coming across one such example while observing the sky at night:

> if the moon is showing on a certain night and it's orange? I might catch it orange? That is *so* sexy to me. And I do not know why. I'm, like, just weird like that . . . like, I don't just see the moon as the moon, like, I know it serves a purpose and all, but I'm just like, "What's going on with the moon . . . ?" Like, "What, whatchu doin'?" If I could have a conversation with it [*laughs*] . . . like, "You just feeling orange today? Okay."

In this case, the aesthetic corporeality exuded by the moon and its particular color triggered a heightened Sensual Pleasure volume for the observer.

Reds and pinks also appear to be sources of visual appeal, serving as both a literal source of exudation and as loud symbolic representations of "lust," passion, boldness or arousal. Sunday, a heterosexual North Carolina woman in her early 20s, recounted a regional representation of the color red that shows up in her current ideations of color and sensual pleasure:

> [s]o, from the South, red lipstick, red nail polish was, like, not allowed, just because, I guess—I think at one point, red was like a black, you know, it was like the sultriness, now it's like black, the black dress. So, I don't know—if you ever see movies, you always see someone in, like, red lipstick or a red dress, so I guess growing up I always associated with, like, being an adult, being a woman, being, like, a sexy, confident woman. Is that—Jessica Rabbit—the movie with Jessica Rabbit—she has on, like, this red skin-tight dress and this red lipstick, and, like, she's a cartoon character. But, um, still it's always that red lip; I don't know why. It's just like, it's just seen as . . . I think it's more of the color than the application of makeup, but it's just . . . red [*laughs*].

Sunday's example raises an important juxtaposition, highlighting the salience of the Erotic Self as chief observer and establisher of sexiness in one's own universe. Even while being discouraged by others during her upbringing, Sunday was still able to establish red as a source of sexiness for herself. Those who attempted to tamper with this element of Sunday's control panel may have been doing so as a means to restrict her alone, or may have been projecting that norm from their own insecurities about wearing red as part of their own sexiness expression. I will speak more in Chapter 6 about how this could potentially emerge.

Going back to Kim's cuddle date example, a person's environment can provide significant sources of aesthetic pleasure even without other visually appealing bodies being present. For some, the nature of a forest or beach provides visual pleasure that is, as Sunday explains, "its rawest form . . . when you can be, like, raw, and not have, like, any type of mask or any type of covering." This could be an additional way of looking at Camille's depiction of the moon; when encountered one could be taken by its color but also by its shape, the dimensions in its face or its brightness and clarity. "Waterfalls," "leaves," "stars," "flowers" and "butterflies" are all reported parts of an unmanipulated outdoor scene that could fit within the realm of aesthetic corporeal exudation that inspires sensual pleasure for an observer.

Touch and sight are significant aspects of sensual pleasure for many, if not most, people among the sample. For several respondents, however, smell and sound are just as significant in creating pleasurable sensory experience.

"Good smelling perfume," "musk," "vanilla" and "citrus" were all examples of smells that triggered sensual pleasure among respondents. For one respondent in particular, complementary body scents, or "scent that melds with mine," were of greater importance than any particular smell itself. Sonically, the sound of laughter is titillating for some; the ability to laugh with another is simultaneously pleasurable to the ears and abdominal muscles. Yoncé, a married, heterosexual woman in Ohio, explained that, for her,

> laughing as hard as I do with my partner can be just as exciting for me as a sexual encounter . . . any type of connection that can be made that would make me genuinely laugh could mean that we could have a connection on many other fronts.

Music is a popular form of aural pleasure as well—perhaps the most varied in the ways it is experienced. Music can be used catalytically, inspiring fantasies of other sensory experiences, providing models of sexiness to emulate (e.g., Cardi B, Megan Thee Stallion) or stoking desires to connect with others sexually. For James, a Louisville, Kentucky, transgender man in his late 20s, the sensory experience of music in particular provides multilayered sensual pleasure, including the physiological benefits of music notes themselves:

> I'm a fan of bass, and I think that I have a physiological reaction to that. I'm a fan specifically of, like, minor notes. Um, I think I have a reaction to that. Um . . . yeah . . . it's both of those things. Like, I mean, music can literally, like, if—I suffer from depression—it can literally put me in a good mood.

There is significant evidence to suggest that pleasure received in the moment from the olfactory and aural senses in particular is both physiological, triggering the release of endorphins and oxytocin (Dunbar, 2004; Janata & Grafton, 2003), and psychological—related to cognitive linkages made between the event and the positive significance assigned to it or the potential establishment of greater closeness between erotic beings (Dunbar, 2004; Duvall et al., 2012).

Not to be outdone by other senses, taste is also a significant source of sensual pleasure for many. Whether it's "salty," "sweet" or "chocolaty," stimulation of the taste buds is a strong indicator of arousal or sensory satisfaction. For some, taste includes the body fluids produced during coital encounters, including sweat, semen and vaginal secretions. For others, savory pleasure can come specifically through certain foods or from the act of eating itself. Samantha in Delaware, whose insights on Erotic Energy were introduced in Chapter 3, shared additional insight about the power of the palate in stimulating taste-based sensual pleasure for her:

> [f]ood! Oh my God, food is so sexy. That's probably like—next to me that's literally, like, the second sexiest thing, like. . . . Food orgasms are real [*laughs*]; I don't care what anyone says, that is a *fact*. . . . Ever since I was a baby, every time I got food, I danced. Like, I just . . . 'cause how else can you express yourself? Like, it just makes you feel good. It just, it makes you warm and tingly inside. Food is love—like, that's just the easiest way to get, like, how—it's love. It's just love. . . . I think it's the experience . . . like, the—what it does to your senses—like, all of them. So not even the physical, just, like, the taste and the smell and the feeling and . . . it's very sensual!

As with other types of sensual pleasure, even the recounting of pleasurable taste experiences can be a sensory experience in itself. In that case the experience would be considered more mental than physically induced (further explained in the next section). Whether it be taste, touch, smell, sight or sound, however, the body and its senses are the fundamental landscape on which sensory experience is most readily identified and accessible.

Mental Excitation

As was noted in Chapter 2, personal growth via self-improvement is an intended aspect of many respondents' sexiness development. Mental Excitation, the second of the sensory experience channels, serves as a significant source for stimulating this process. It is the excitation aspect of this channel that makes it a sensory experience; the feeling of enlightenment created by a mental encounter is experienced by the observer like the turning of a switch in the brain—a flicker from subconscious to new, conscious energy. These flickers originate in the mind (e.g., an "A-ha Moment") and then connect with physiological occurrences in other parts of the body (e.g., increased heart rate, goosebumps, genital arousal), as it awakens to the perceived implications of the stimuli in question. The two emergent forms of Mental Excitation identified among this sample were *intelligence* and *fantasy*.

On its own, possessing the capacity to inspire mental sparks could be viewed as a type of comportment, describing people who are curious or inquisitive. In this case, however, mental excitation most stemmed from the actions believed to represent "intelligence"—exhibited "smarts" or "intellect" that results in stimulating new or advanced types of thinking for the observer in question. One respondent spoke about the pleasure of "geeking out on fantasy or anime" with someone—another, the inspiration of engaging with "an avid reader." Denise in Detroit, Michigan, spoke of intelligence as a type of sexiness enhancer for someone of interest by sharing that "there'll be times when I hear someone speak, and that changes how I look at them . . . that sexiness comes in like, 'Oh shit; he actually knows something . . .'" Particularly if, as in this case, the expression of intelligence is unexpected, mental excitation can enhance the perceived exudation volume level coming from the observed erotic being.

An observer having an experience of mental excitation can experience varying feelings of contentment, euphoria and personal motivation. Jerome's experience of this channel was pleasurable even in recollection. He recounted, "Intelligence is like, 'Whoo!' [*laughing*]. Nothing like it." For 40-year-old Crystal in Chicago, intellect is a subtle yet palpable sense of relational fit where both she and her romantic/sexual partner experience "this cerebral thing where if we hit it off intellectually, then everything else sort of falls into place." Thirty-something Olive in Philadelphia described feeling a vigorous kinetic stimulation from her intellectual exchanges:

> [intelligence] challenges me . . . someone that's, like, smart and intelligent and is . . . conscious about things that are going on . . . we can have, like, dialogue, and you can challenge me on, you know, my thoughts and have, like, an intelligent back and forth and debate.

Though debate is not necessarily part of her experiences, 58-year old Sephra related a sense of edification when she described intellect as "feeding me. It's feeding me . . . it's feeding the inner portion of myself that needs to be fed . . ." In perhaps an even deeper mental excitation experience, Evelyn referred to a conversation she had while on a particular date as "being in a trance":

> [l]ike, I literally could see myself have a future with this person. It was like we were "simpatico." And it was like they were speaking and I could hear what they were saying, but I could imagine a future we could have together. I was projecting what could be.

In Evelyn's case, intellect mixed with her imagination to produce a full on fantasy that pleased her mind and body simultaneously. Fantasy is further reviewed later; however, in all of these cases, intelligence emerged as a type of mental excitation in which the brain was directly stimulated, resulting in various sensations felt throughout the body both inside and outside of each particular moment when the excitation took place.

Fantasy is the second area of mental excitation in which an individual may experience arousal, attraction or sexiness development. Whether it is an erotic being we desire, a confident celebrity we wish to emulate or sexual outcome or sequence of sexual events we hope to see play out, individuals can find sexiness in mentally conjuring up images that represent the ideal imaginary world of their design. Katherine, a queer 20-something-year-old in New Jersey, discussed using fantasy during her early stages of comportment development—a tool she still finds useful in navigating sensory experiences in the present:

> [g]rowing up, I was always, like, a very introverted person. Like, I'm less so now, but when I was younger. And when I was a child I was, like, really, really shy. And that's a big part of why I'm drawn to, like, things that help me to imagine more than actually communicate directly. It's just easier for me to think of things first and visualize that first before I take physical action. And that kinda, like, spills over a lot with, like, my sexual life now; I kinda like to try things out in my head first and then get a feel of, like, how do I feel about this emotionally and, like, does this feel comfortable for me and then acting on it.

In Katherine's specific case, fan fiction is a major source of fantasy conceptualization for her; for others, it might be songs, romantic novels or movies—even pornography.

What is perhaps most exemplified by Katherine's story is the idea that while some fantasies can be experienced simply for mental excitation's sake, others can serve as possibility models for experiences and activities that are eventually carried out in one's external life, leading to subsequent sensual pleasures. Though this is possible, a fantasy being carried out externally is not guaranteed, nor is it required for a sensory experience to have occurred for the observer. If they do become externalized, the dimensions and details of one's fantasies can be but are also not determinative of what they may look like when they are enacted externally. It is most likely that an individual will enact their fantasies relative to the level of desire or capacity they have to do so. In this way, it is most up to the erotic self in question whether a fantasy is enacted in the outside world.

Ultimately, whether the result is a greater sense of satisfaction with the world, a greater vision of a future with other erotic beings or greater sense of attraction to the erotic beings with which we relate, mental excitation is a sensory experience that can provide cognitive, emotional and physiological stimulation both in the moment and thereafter.

Relationship

As has been previously noted, sexiness requires only one observer to be adequately assessed as such. That said, sexiness is often sought and found in the intentional connections we make with others in whom we have erotic interest. Relationships in the BSE model refer to the specific energetic arrangements made between erotic beings as well as the actions that take place within those connections. They may come with official titles representing formal associations (e.g., "lovers," "spouses," "parent/child," "siblings") or they may be temporary creations, forged through time-specific contexts like weekend retreats or one-night stands. Individuals may assess sexiness in relationships they are in with the exuded beings they find themselves attracted to or in the relationships said beings have with others, including family, friends and other lovers. Emergent qualities of relationship sexiness reported by individuals in this study include connection, acts of service, reciprocity and communication.

For many, feeling *connection* with others is a significant sensory experience, if not an inextricable part of one's whole sexuality. Many respondents reported valuing the ability to feel connected to the exuded beings that attract them—to experience a particular emotional intimacy that supersedes general self/other awareness. Connection can be a gateway to sensual pleasure, as Aaron, discussed in Chapter 3, noted is their preference: "you can't have sex without it, but you can have it without sex." Connection and chemistry, an equivalent terms used by respondents, both have close relationships to erotic energy via the theme of attraction discussed in Chapter 3. For all three concepts—connection, chemistry and erotic energy—participants described the experience of either being an observer drawn to an erotic being or witnessing two erotic selves being drawn to each other. All that said, connection in this case speaks more to the ways individuals fit relationally with the exuded beings in their lives than to the essence of the fit itself. Within this notion lies a deeper sense of intimate knowing—an awareness that is often imperceptible to even those involved. Elle in Detroit cited the experience of being out in public with an individual with whom one experiences this type of relating: "it's just like, 'Yeah.' You lock eyes across the room, and it's just like, 'Yeah' [snaps]. 'Yeah. I know you, you know me, like, we got this down.'"

"Vulnerability" and "emotional risk-taking" are other reported ideas fitting within the theme of connection. At least one member of the sample described sexiness as being able to "close your eyes to feel pleasurable sensations without fear," directly implicating trust and vulnerability as integral aspects of connection building. Samantha in Delaware echoed a similar sentiment both regarding her own sexiness journey and as a general principle:

> I like how I feel when I'm allowed to be vulnerable . . . safe. Safe . . . you have to be able to be vulnerable with your partner, I feel like. You have to. I've definitely—thinking back on different times I've had sex where I wasn't vulnerable with somebody or didn't trust them to be vulnerable with them versus a person that I did trust to be vulnerable with. Two totally different contacts; like, they're two completely different times.

To say that emotional vulnerability is a fundamental part of relationship experience is not to suggest it is required to the degree Samantha suggests. The willingness to prioritize vulnerability within one's relationship, however, appears to provide an opportunity for significant emotional and erotic satisfaction. Kim in Washington, D.C., provided another example involving cuddle dates:

> [t]his [erotic encounter] is the space where we can be vulnerable because obviously we're gonna have some type of conversations. You're nearby me and cuddling. I can hold you if you're, um, disclosing things that make you feel some type of way or put you in a certain type of space. I can hold you and put you into a space where you can begin to heal.

Though not a prerequisite, again, connection often appears to occur in moments of emotional vulnerability where individuals take risks to reveal their deeper selves and are then received with kindness and emotional holding space by those they are in relationship with.

Individuals who have opened themselves up to other erotic beings do so primarily with the intention of experiencing particular relationship-based activities, including caretaking (e.g., showing concern for one's welfare) and elevated status (e.g., transitioning from casual acquaintance to committed partner). Coital activities may also occur as a result of connections that are built, though they are not required and often, particularly in the case of familial-based connections, may not be intended. Ryann, a queer asexual woman in her late 20s, spoke about the ways connection helps her differentiate between the attention she receives from platonic significant others and that she may get from strangers:

> [w]hen my best friends say, "Ryann you are beautiful, Ryann, you are fine, you are sexy"—all these things? Um, and they're saying it in a very, like, if it can be said, in a very platonic way? I think to myself, "We have an intimate connection where you know me, and so I can receive that from you because you see me." Um, but a man catcalling me on the street I'm like [*sucks teeth*], "Cut that off. You don't deserve that part of me, and I don't wanna—I don't want you seeing me in that light." I don't want to be a sex symbol or sex item or object to anyone because I am a person. And when I do decide to engage in my sexuality, it's because I feel safe with the intimacy [connection] we have created.

As Ryann's example shows, connection can help to moderate boundaries between what an individual deems offensive behavior and what they consider attractive comportment. Denise in Detroit reiterated this sentiment during our conversation by noting that, in her opinion, "Closeness . . . that can override almost anything."

As was noted in the last chapter, people may find themselves drawn to erotic beings exhibiting compassionate comportment, who are mindful of and attentive to the needs of others. In relationships, compassion may be more likely assessed while experiencing *acts of service* provided by loved ones and significant others. Any type of behavior that involves an individual going out of their way to accommodate the needs or desires of another, whether solicited or unsolicited, can be considered an act of service in this model. While the most recognizable gifts may be sensual activities, such as drawing a bath, preparing a meal or giving someone fellatio or cunnilingus, unsolicited gifts and words of affirmation may also be included in this category. Acts of service need not be directed at the observer to be considered sexiness and can be experienced as a service to one's self (or potential service) by proxy. As Yoncé in Ohio noted,

> For me, being able to see you take care of somebody that you love is extremely sexy for me because ultimately you also love me, so if you can take care of your family like that, ideally you would be able to take care of somebody else that you love—that you're dating or that you're married to or that you're—whatever, in courtship with, whatever you want to say, in the same vein.

Given the elevated status of certain relationships over others, an act of service may make an individual feel as if they are receiving preferential treatment by the giver. These acts may also give implicit permission for the recipient to relinquish any obligation they feel to privilege others' needs over their own—a particular benefit for individuals who regularly serve in other areas of their lives. Lola was one of several femme-identified folks who raised this point:

> I feel like, for me, a lot of the times I feel like I'm doing a lot of the work. So it's nice when I don't have to do a lot of the work and they don't expect me to do a lot of the work. So that's always nice.

Indeed, the ability to pamper, whether physically or emotionally, can be a particularly appreciated act of service for the way it allows the recipient to relinquish responsibility in the moment.

Though relationship through acts of service may be perceived by some as the chance to renounce responsibility in the negotiation and carrying out of sensory experiences, others may be more eager to both give and receive in their relationships. These are individuals for whom *reciprocity* would be of greater importance—not to be burdened with the bulk of effort required for cultivating sexiness within the relationship, though not to necessarily give up the opportunity to serve or please either. Clarke, a heterosexual woman in North Carolina, described reciprocity as "[b]eing a sexual equal—where we're kinda in the same place . . . not one is too far ahead, one is too far back, you know—we're kinda in the same place when it comes to that." This aspect of being in the same place could be in experience, action, attitude and a variety of other factors. Luna in Philadelphia pointed out that her history with lovers who received pleasure more than they were willing to give it inspired her desire for more reciprocal service during sexual encounters: "I'm not really expecting much, like, on the receiving end [*laughs*]. But also I just, like, really enjoy giving and . . . I want the other person to be that enthusiastic about it as well." For Darius, a gay man in the Midwest, reciprocity of enthusiasm was equally important. As he explained,

> I've been in scenarios where I'm the only one doing all the work and they're just kind of lazy or laying there, and I stop because if you're just lying there I feel like I'm raping you because you're not participating. That creeps me out.

For Lanaya in Detroit, reciprocity emerges as a particularly comprehensive goal of sorts, covering different types of relationships:

> [e]ven just having a casual friendship or a casual encounter [or a] friends with benefits situation, just, in my view, sexiness, just, when you meet someone and they decide, yes, I would like to spend some amount of my time, some amount of my ability to be open and vulnerable with another person—even if it's just, like, in a very diminished capacity . . . just, like, having the ability to open yourself up and be accepting of someone else's vulnerability, to me, is what sexiness is.

Reciprocity has the capacity to cover a wide range of relationship expectations regarding attitudes, behaviors and experiences. Individuals seeking reciprocity ultimately look for relating styles or encounters that provide a good balance of give-and-take behaviors and a general sense of mutuality regarding one's feelings and intentions.

For some individuals, perceptions of connection are mostly gained through observing unspoken actions, which are then implicitly decoded for their significance by the observer. For others, however, relationship is established through active verbal communication, with sexiness being assessed more readily from that. Aaron in Philadelphia expressed a common challenge in this regard, asserting that a lack of willful, stimulating communication from attractive exuded beings often deterred them from finding quality relationships and opportunities for sensual activity. As they noted during our conversation, "[I]t's kinda like, 'Well, yeah, we can do that. We can always do that. But can, can we have a conversation? And a lot of times, that's not the case." For them and other folks, like Maria in Buffalo, New York, the ability to verbally reason with significant others is the foundation of a good partnership and, by extension, good sexual encounters. Showing thoughtfulness, ease and consistency in the way one speaks, along with actively listening and effectively integrating information received from others, provides a quality sensory experience for individuals for whom communication matters, regardless of the conversation's subject matter. In fact, such behavior can serve as a model for other individuals looking to improve their communication capacity. For example, Zephra in Milwaukee, Wisconsin, noted that, for her, a potential lover should "[c]ommunicate to me. Teach me how to be a better communicator," adding that, "I think that's one of my most flawed parts: I don't communicate as well as I'd like to." Ideally, then, good communication serves as a bridge between parties that can facilitate a number of sensory experiences, including ones on other channels (e.g., mental excitation, positive affect).

One final point to reiterate about relationships as a sexiness channel involves the ways that individuals use relationship and its emergent dimensions to access other sexiness channels in ways they might not see themselves as able to do otherwise. Alaia, a heterosexual Atlanta femme in her mid-20s, notes that "there's some things that I'll mention in certain groups where I'm comfortable expressing my sexuality or being more sexually expressive with certain groups of people than I probably would with other individuals." Hers is an example of how intentionally increased access to this channel in particular can result in opportunities to increase volume in sexiness channels that may otherwise go silenced. For Elizabeth in Washington, D.C., relationships built through a segregated emotional safe space have been integral to affirming her erotic self and generating sexiness development:

> it's funny because I really do ... it's not like I lead a double life, although I do know that's a strange way to intro that. But, um ... I definitely have, sort of, distinct circles in my life now. And so I still manage to surround myself with, like, lots of lovely, bookish, nerdy, awesome people, most of whom are also connected to the queer community in some way, a fair number of whom are connected to, like, kink communities and, like, BDSM communities and, like, just poly communities—all of these different variations on like, gender and sexual identities.... I've been very lucky that eventually when I decided to kind of come out to a fair number or people as, like ... queer is my umbrella identifier ... it's connected me with such a great network of people that I like, love and crave—these people that are not just in these moments. But that are also observing and recording and understanding and dissecting and, like, analyzing these moments ... to me, it's, um, allowed me to sorta find sexy space in the bookishness about all of this and having these kinds of risqué, um, like, conversations and experiences with other people who are on that same spectrum, who have these very ... there's [work] space for me where I'm really sorta policing myself and my interactions and my appearance, and then, I like, you know, I spend, like, half of my summer weekends in New York ... essentially I get to be with a group of people that's just like, so open and free, and people are just, like, living out loud with abandon, and it's a very central space ...

Driving the point home again with both Alaia's and Elizabeth's cases, individuals may receive sensory experience through relationship in at least two main ways: the specific activities they engage in with other individuals through their affinitive connections and the emotional boost of validation they receive accessing the freedom provided within and by those safe, affirming spaces.

Positive Affect

It should almost go without saying that people enjoy sensory experiences because of how good they make them feel—physically, emotionally or otherwise. That said, there is also a meta-level of emotional experience that can serve as its own sensory experience. In layman's terms, people like to feel good, and they also enjoy and are drawn to the *feeling of* feeling good. This latter point is the most fundamental aspect of Positive Affect within the BSE model; relatedly, however, it also refers to the internal physiological responses one may sense as part of their emotions. Cole, a heterosexual man in his late 40s, described an example of Positive Affect in action when he asserted, "You can tell people that are generally happy because of something; it's almost like an aura because it comes from the inside and shines out." In this example, the whole body is perceived to be both feeling and radiating this emotion, which results in the observer feeling an equivalent level of happiness within his own body. Stories similar to these were noted throughout several other points during the study, all of which related back to respondents' descriptions of sexiness.

"Love," "happiness," "affection" and "pride" were a few reported emotions linked to sexiness by individuals within the sample. These were emotions felt about one's self, the objects one owned, a relationship or the erotic beings or experience encountered within one's relationship. Brynda, a Philadelphia woman in her early 20s, noted the relationship between Positive Affect and Comportment, stating that "once people become— once they own their sexuality, once they have that freedom, there's a kind of happiness that comes with that." Freddie, a homosexual man in Washington, D.C., explained the role of affect in his conceptualizations of sexiness, noting that for him sexiness was "me and a friend trying to get to know each other in a happy and joyful and excited way." Stated again, people appeared to have both real-time and reverberating experiences of positive affect first while being drawn to people who felt good emotionally to them and then while observing their willingness to exude that emotionality to others.

In some ways, descriptions of the physiological aspects inherent in Positive Affect feel reminiscent of Erotic Energy and may share a connection in this regard. Moreover, Positive Affect appears able to provide a backdrop for more fully experiencing other channels, including Relationship, given its dimension of emotional vulnerability. For those willing to take the risk, the simultaneous pursuit of Positive Affect with this particular sensory experience may result in complementary increases in one's erotic energy exudation and relationship sensory volumes, leading to an increase in one's sexiness development overall.

To conclude, the Eight Channels of Sexiness describe a myriad of characteristics, attitudes, behaviors, ideas and experiences. Each channel has the capacity to operate alone, though they most often transmit their frequencies in combination with each other according to an individual's unique lived experience. It is the Erotic Self who determines the sexiness channels that are most relevant to their lives along with the volumes and frequencies they wish to see transmitted through them. Let us now turn to a discussion of this central actor within the BSE model.

Note

1 Use of the term *healthy* here reflects colloquial connotations of physical fortitude associated with body thickness and not any traditional medical use of the term.

References

Brown Douglas, K. (1999). *Sexuality and the black church: A womanist perspective*. Maryknoll, NY: Orbis Books.

Descartes, R., & Voss, S. (1989). *The passions of the soul*. Indianapolis: Hackett Publishing Company.

Dunbar, R. I. M. (2004). *The human story*. London: Faber and Faber.

Duvall, J. L., Oser, C. B., Mooney, J., Staton-Tindall, M., Havens, J. R., & Leukefeld, C. G. (2012). Feeling good in your own skin: The influence of complimentary sexual stereotypes on risky sexual attitudes and behaviors in a community sample of African American women. *Women & Health, 53*(1), 1–19. https://doi.org/10.1080/03630242.2012.750260

Janata, P., & Grafton, S. T. (2003). Swinging in the brain: Shared neural substrates for behaviors related to sequencing and music. *Nature Neuroscience, 6*, 682–687. https://doi.org/10.1038/nn1081

5
THE EROTIC SELF

TONY'S STORY

Tony is a single 41-year-old man living in Philadelphia, Pennsylvania. He's a regional rail conductor who has had, up until recently, a robust and pleasurable sex life. Born and raised in the Germantown section of the city, Tony had access to sex and pleasure early on in his life, beginning with a sexual experience with the 35-year-old he "lost [his] virginity to" at age 14. When it first happened, Tony wasn't sure what to think of his experience; after reporting it to his uncle and male cousins, however, their positive reaction made him consider the encounter a good thing, and as such he proceeded to continue having and enjoying sex with other women and girls accordingly—always making sure to use a condom for every encounter and avoiding anything additional that would put him at risk of experiencing an unwanted pregnancy or sexually transmitted infection.

One of the things Tony's first "partner" lauded him for was the size of his penis. As he got older he learned that having a large penis was expected of him as a Black man, as was being good at pleasing women sexually, engaging in as much *sex as he could get and being ready for sex at any moment the opportunity was made available to him. This perspective served Tony in his adulthood until age 37, when a simultaneous car accident and diagnosis of hypertension affected both his sexual desire and his overall erectile capacity. The experience triggered a deep depression in Tony, as his inability to perform to previous standards caused him to question his identity as a man and shook his confidence in his ability to attract the same caliber of sexual partners he once had and to maintain the same level of sexual pleasure he once knew. Adding insult to injury, Tony now finds himself challenged in his capacity to discuss his emotional difficulties with others, as his main line to emotional connection occurred through the sexual connections he made with his female partners, many of whom he now avoids out of fear of losing their respect and thus his reputation.*

As was established in Chapter 2, few to no individuals in this study talked about sexuality being a universe in ways that did not include themselves. This sense of self, the Erotic Self, was most acutely described as not only an aspect of one's sexuality but also one's chief sexual actor and conceptual orchestrator. In the same way a sound engineer organizes selected sounds and frequencies into a mastered final soundtrack, the Erotic Self applies one's interests and aspirations toward mastering a unique sexual expression, one that feels most accessible and authentic to them. Moving toward mastery in practice can look like a wide range of activities, establishing the desired channels of sexiness one wishes to work with, establishing how much of each sexiness signal one will exude or experience and, when useful, negotiating opportunities for exudation or enjoying sensory experiences with others. To be clear, there is no authentic sexuality within the present model that does not include an awareness of one's own Erotic Self, as participants were clear that no one can legitimately determine what sexiness/sexuality should be for anyone else *except* themselves. Establishment of this relationship is what makes the Erotic Self the most important entity within the BSE model.

While the original intention of this research was not focused in this particular way, Erotic Self persisted as an emergent concept throughout most of the study, which is why it has been given its own chapter for discussion. That said, given its tangential relationship to the initial research topic, it is not clear from this sample whether the themes mentioned here fulfill the extent of personalities available to the Erotic Self or if establishment of a definitive list of erotic personas is even possible.[1] The following six descriptions reflect the diversity found within this particular sample and highlight the established vantage points through which these individuals engage with their control panel. Briefly, each of the following personas exemplifies how various Erotic Selves go about engineering sexiness and cognitively processing what sexiness means to them. Erotic personas were organized into three main types, representing the perceiving source emphasized by the respondent. For example, the vast majority of respondents described themselves in ways that I coded as either "Doer/Be-er" or "Journeyer" or "Relator." I classified these personas as "subjective" to reflect how they represent the individual's reliance on their own self-perception. Two additional personas, "Magnet" and "Product," emerged from individuals whose self-perception reflected a reliance on the impressions of others; these received an "objective" classification. Finally, the erotic self-persona of "Sexual Brand" was given a "neutral" designation, being capable of both subjectivity and objectivity. To reiterate, the terms established for Erotic Self personas in this model are preliminary and descriptive. In addition, none of these descriptions are mutually exclusive, having the capacity to overlap contextually, much like the Eight Channels. The remainder of the chapter discusses each of the six Erotic Self personas in more detail.

Doer/Be-er

One need not actively think about one's Erotic Self to embody it. For the "Doer," sexiness is a function of their actions and activities. When talking about their erotic selves, doers speak most often of their sensual activities, assessing the quality, diversity or number of their accomplishments or pleasure experienced through them. If Doers are having satisfying sensory pleasures (most often sexual intercourse), then they perceive themselves as experiencing optimal sexiness. Theo, a married heterosexual man in his 40s, represents a quintessential doer in his self-assessment as a "participant":

> I'm engaged in it with my wife, you know, and it's fulfilling because it has more meanings than just [sex] for me . . . it can be a spiritual feeling; it can be . . . kind of whimsical; it can be anything. . . . That's what I see myself as.

"Be-ers" are like Doers in their lack of active thought around the Erotic Self. For the Be-er, however, sexiness is simply an inherent aspect of their overall sense of self, outside of one's actions or behaviors. Octavia in Buffalo, New York, could be best described as a Be-er when reviewing how she describes others' assessment of her exuded being: "I don't look at myself as being sexy. I am who I am every day." For the Be-er, sexiness is most often discussed as the individual's present exuded being, whether assessed by others or one's own self. In this case, optimal sexiness is perceivably achieved when the individual's exudation volume is strongest yet most humble, authentic and unforced. Camila in Buffalo, New York, shared more from this perspective:

> [p]eople that I've connected to that I consider sexy, like, to me it's hard to explain, but it's almost like organic in a way. It's, like, nothing that's forced, [it's not] like I'm trying to make you be this sexy person. Like, if you're just being yourself and your personality or whatever it is that makes you you turns me on? Then that's usually, like, the best scenario for me, as opposed to me tryna ask all these, you know, questions about you, you know. You're coming up with answers, but your intent is either to impress me or tell me what I want to hear or whatever . . . that affects whether or not I think you're sexy.

Camila's self-description would fit more of a Journeyer (to be described later); however, her desire to engage with a Be-er persona exemplifies how self- and other-assessment may not be identical.

Doers and Be-ers are not mutually exclusive. Victoria, a heterosexual woman in her early 30s, exhibited examples of both Doer and Be-er energy in her self-assessment as well as a bit of Relator:

> I'm sexy [laughs]. I mean . . . honestly? . . . In my personal life, I like to think that I'm sexy. I like to think that I'm good at [having sex], and it's, in a relationship, it's an important part to me.

Victoria establishes herself as a Be-er via self-assessment of her own exuded being and as a Doer by virtue of her assessed sexual skill set and the prioritization of sexual intercourse in her romantic relationships. Though she does not expound on it, she ends her statement by alluding to her capacity as a relator as well, which is described later. Note that none of these are aspects of herself that she shares in a boasting or performative way; they are offered matter-of-factly, in a way more reflective of self-description

Journeyer

Journeyers, by and large, see themselves on a path of or toward sexiness, either acquiring initial access to it through exudation and sensory experience or building on previous achievements. These individuals most commonly refer to sexuality as being on a "journey," or with the use of other travel- or evolution-based language (e.g., "becoming," "evolving"). The journey toward sexiness may include a number of processing activities, including working through previous traumas or sexual conservatism in their upbringing. In the case of Lalah, a Washington, D.C., woman in her 50s, the journey was heavily informed by early constrictive social norms:

> I think that, growing up, especially when I grew up, there were so many taboos around sex, and I was that fast little girl who was considered—you know, I was looking at boys when I was five and six years old. And, uh, and I did not understand why I was being called that, necessarily. Um, I do now. I understand now that, um, I came into my own sexual identity as a girl because I *did* like boys at five. . . . My ideas about sex and sexuality have evolved, and I've allowed myself to be freer about my attitudes about sex.

The steps in Lalah's journey, as she related them, involved releasing the judgments projected onto her by others in her early environment while simultaneously moving toward a self-validated embrace of sexiness—particularly sensual pleasure and erotic attraction.

Desiring to advance or perceiving one's self as incomplete in its sexiness development does not preclude an individual from being able to experience exuded being or sensory experience in the immediate moment. In this case, the Journeyer is both present and forward thinking about their development trajectory, often seeing gradual improvement as an integral part of the process. Grace, a heterosexual young adult in Detroit, and Greg, a middle-aged gay man in Atlanta, both understood their ability to overcome challenges as being part of their respective evolution toward increased sexiness:

> [i]t's very interesting to see who I am now and who I used to be and even thoughts I had about my own sexuality and other people's sexuality. And it's—in *many* instances it's just very different. So I guess I like

that idea of . . . like, a divorcing [of old ideas] and coming of age, kind of, for me.

(Grace)

I think I have, over the years, become more, um . . . more adult about my ideas of what, who I am in the world. Who I am in . . . my space, as far as being able to, uh, look at what I have to offer as a person, look at what makes me happy, and being able to express that to the person I wanna get to know.

(Greg)

On a rudimentary level, Journeyers will often use sexiness development to grow as an erotic being or to grow in understanding their sexual universe. In some cases, they have not yet determined the type of exuded being or sensory experiences they want in the present moment, nor have they had encounters that put them in tune with their console's full capabilities. Gaberial, a 19-year-old college student living in Brooklyn, indicated as much when describing the birth of her relationship to sexiness:

> it's funny enough because, like, I was just thinking this the other day too. So, um, I . . . don't consider myself a sexy person. Like, I'm trying to be in a little way. Like, 'cause . . . I was the fat kid [growing up]. So, like, any image anyone ever had of me was solely on my weight . . . and so recently, like, puberty happened, so I grew a couple inches and shimmied [sic] down a bit, and my mom was like, "Oh, this is nice!" and everyone was like "Oh, you look so sexy!" . . . so I'm just like, "Okay [*laughs*]! What is this word?" I've never attributed it to myself. So, like, sometimes I'll just be like, "Okay, let's try to find sexiness . . ."

Wherever they intend to end it, Journeyers experience their erotic self at various stages of travel: just approaching the start of their development journey, sometimes making their way along at a steady place ("my sexiness is an interstate"), experiencing intentional or unexpected stagnancy at parts ("right now I'd say I don't") or looking back over previous years to reflect on the overall sexiness journey ("I'm really, really boring . . . because I've tried so many things").

Relator

The last of the subjective erotic selves, the Relator, describes individuals whose sense of erotic self is primarily, and in some cases inextricably, linked to other individuals with whom they share sensory experiences. For example, while other elements in her universe carry some additional weight, Crystal in Chicago noted that "long-term sexiness has always been about how I relate to this other person, how they come off to me—like, how *they* are, on the inside" (italics mine). Carlton in Milwaukee noted "relatability" as a primary source of sexiness for him, clarifying that "[n]o one wants to be with someone they can't relate to, who can't understand the things they've been through." Jasmine, a 30-something queer sexuality educator in New York, described themself as a Relator on a deeper emotional level:

> I think personally, for me, sexuality has always been something very intimate. It's not a one-off. It's a very, like, "We are coming together and this is gonna be something that we're doing for a while." Um . . . and even in our conversation, it's gonna be sexual.

For respondents like Freddie, discussed in Chapter 4, relationship is fundamental to the erotic self-concept:

> [I see myself in sexuality by] knowing that I'm a good person, and [that] I try to find another good person like me who understands me and my baggage and who's there for me and [who I know has my back.]

In many cases, it is the individual's ability to better relate or be involved in optimal relationship that most shapes their exuded being and determines the quality of their sensory experience.

For some Relators, sexiness is enhanced by one's ability to exude or enhance sensory experience within relationships. Cree, a Midwest heterosexual woman in her late 30s, noted that "for me, in my relationships I am an affectionate person, too, and I am a nurturer too. I like my partner to feel like they're loved." Lola, a young woman living on the East Coast, pointed out that, for her, having a sexuality that centers her is "opposite of what I am literally. I think I'm a very, uh, people pleaser. So, like . . . specifically, with partners, I will go out of my way to do whatever I can to please them sexually." This particular type of Relator persona could also be seen as a hybrid Relator-Doer, with a greater emphasis on Relationship as the Sensory Experience channel being accessed.

It seems that, generally speaking, the Relator may not prioritize their own sexual autonomy and may even perceive a less emphasized sense of personal sexiness when they are not in a relationship. Cleopatra spoke to this dynamic and explained its effects on her sense of personal exuded being:

> [r]ight now in my life . . . I haven't been that in tune with my life, in terms of my desires, needs and wants as far as sex goes. . . . I think about my sexuality as far as, like, my identity and things like that because you gotta know what you're looking for in order to get intimacy. But as far as everything else . . . I dunno, I just don't take myself into consideration. I only really use sexuality to talk about other people.

In this case, Cleopatra's awareness of the capacity she has to develop sexiness by herself appears diminished by her focus on others. That said, while it may be easy to assume that Relators compromise parts of their sexiness by centering others, what may also follow is the possibility that prioritizing partnership or one's relationship partner may actually enhance personal sexiness, and specifically Exuded Being, through confidence extended from the Comportment channel.

Magnet

Magnets are the first of the subjective personas and refer to individuals who see and utilize their erotic self as a tool for drawing others to them (and vice versa). For these respondents, sexiness development is often the quest to increase one's capacity to garner that particular outside attention. This attraction can be acquired through exuding that which matches or is most complementary to what the intended recipient desires. Taquaan, introduced in Chapter 3, returns here with this example:

> [e]verything from chest hair to when I get a shave, when I get a haircut . . . part of my sexuality comes from the opposite sex, on how they look at me and how they, uh, either touch or, or see me.

Other examples of Magnet-type statements among respondents included:

> I think I have the things I like in other women. (Carmen)
> I don't think of how I see myself. . . . I only think of what I'm attracted to. (Jim)
> I guess I've been told a few times that I'm sexy, so I think about what the other person might find sexy in me and the things I embody. (Lola)

Jim, a cisgender, heterosexual Philadelphian in his 30s, gained a significant understanding of himself as a Magnet through his upbringing, which he—coincidentally—also noted as being racialized:

Me: Do you feel like being Black affects the way you think about sex and/or sexuality or experience that?

Jim: Yes. Mm-hmm.

Me: Yeah? Would you say more about that?

Jim: Yeah, so, like, um . . . like, coming up, I think it's, like, generally, we're taught that the more women you can get or the more women you can have is, like, your mark to manhood. Like, I can remember being interested in sex very early. I never had, like, an "Ugh, yucky girl" stage because it was always "You're to be attracted to women. What you do and how you carry yourself is for women."

Me: So the whole way you behaved was about performing for women?

Jim: Oh yeah, oh yeah. . . . If I'm fighting, I'm showing off for the girls that's watching. If I'm playing football it's, you know what I mean, it's to catch an eye . . .

Though he did not explain how this experience might be different for cisgender heterosexual men who were not Black, Jim's ultimate awareness of his own erotic self was tied inextricably to race and a particular type of heterocentric magnetism.

While both masculine and feminine respondents expressed sentiments fitting the Magnet description, femme and female-identified respondents appeared to have a particularly unique experience of being socialized into this type of erotic self given the ways that female sexuality is filtered through society's male gaze. Femme-identified individuals who wish to be Magnets may find it difficult to assert this desire in a way that feels true to them based on what they have been taught to think about female sexuality. Leslie, a married 30-something woman in Maryland, indicated feeling "weird" when considering her own Magnet aspirations, noting that

> when I was growing up, girls who were, like, who maybe showed more skin or who wore a lot of makeup before a certain age or, like, had a sexy body—or, like, a grown person's body, like, so often those girls were written off as being fast or, like, being somehow without morals. And, like, you know, because of that it's often been really hard to figure out or to navigate, you know, being sexy or doing sexy things because, like, you know, there's still some kind of—I still, I think to a certain level, I still have a bit of a hang up with it. Um, when I intentionally try to be sexy it feels fake still, um, so I try not to intentionally do it. Like, I try not to be—I try not to try to do sexy things . . . just 'cause it feels put on a bit.

In this example, Leslie desires to be a Magnet when it comes to her personal exudation but struggles with how to do that authentically because she's been taught to see outward expressions of femme exuded being in such a negative way. While it appears then that both cisgender men and women are socialized into binary magnet expectations, female socialization appears to emphasize sexiness deterrence versus adherence.

Lanaya, a transgender, genderqueer femme in Detroit, emerged as an intersectional type of femme-identified Magnet identity. Throughout our conversation, Lanaya spoke about how the effects of transphobia often resulted in her seeing herself only through the sexiness lenses of others and seeing her sexiness as specifically determined by whether or not someone else expressed interest in having sex. As she put it, "I've never really viewed myself as sexy. I've always, kind of, viewed other people under that lens, just because it's been difficult for me to view myself that way." While Lanaya has grown to actively express her queerness in resistance to society's marginalizing treatment, she still includes magnetism as a significant aspect of her erotic self, noting the perspective that

> [a] lot of times, when we dress certain ways, it's first and foremost for ourselves. But we also want people to look at us and go, "Oh, I like that!" you know? So I want people to look at me and then say, "Oh, I like

that outfit," or, "Oh, I like that hair with that outfit," or, "I like the way they did their makeup." That kind of thing. But also, ideally, especially now . . . I guess my ulterior motive would be—I would like people to look at me and question what gender I am.

Magnets may be seen by some as looking for approval from others that is unnecessary or superficial. In a case like Lanaya's, however, asserting the erotic self as a Magnet could be an important mechanism in pushing past restrictive or oppressive social conventions, particularly those around gender identity and gender expression.

Product

Products might be best described as entities that have been commodified as erotic for the purposes of public consumption or acquisition of capital, both social and material. While they are like Magnets, in that both relate to the subjective attractions of others, Products are usually established as such by those others, occasionally in conflict with the Product's own self-assessment. Products most commonly identify inanimate objects that have been associated with sexiness, particularly those with popular brand names (e.g., "Corvette," "Victoria's Secret"), versus general categories and characteristics (e.g., cars, loungewear). The Product persona, however, may also apply to human beings. Nickie, a North Carolina woman in her early 30s, provided a clear example of how commercialism has affected her own self-awareness as a Product:

> I feel like—as a woman—I feel like I fall into that category of being expected to be sexy all the time. And I feel like that also goes to, like, commercialism, marketing, you know. You have Victoria's Secret, you have, you know, all those different companies that are trying to promote sex and promote sexuality. And I think it draws on women's figures and women's bodies mostly used as objects in order to sell something because sex sells. And so I think I definitely fall into that category, as a woman, falling into that pressure to be sexy.

Nickie's use of the term *pressure* implies that there may be some reluctance on her part to see herself as a Magnet or more interested in garnering attraction. In her case, the pressure of the marketplace creates an expectation that she must spend money to acquire a particular form of exudation that, by extension, increases her accessibility to others—namely, cisgender, heterosexual men. Through the commercial matrix she describes, Nickie is unable to decide for herself if this expectation fits her own organic desires or if she even has organic desires of her own. Many of Nickie's responses during our interview supported a strong awareness of this market influence on the individual's conceptualization of both sexiness and sexuality, such that while she acknowledged that fundamentally "there's something past all of this," she struggled with being able to adequately explain it, citing the market as the strongest inhibiting factor. More on this will be shared in the next chapter.

Femme-identified individuals have a somewhat unique position of being coded as Products by others based on how their bodies are perceived or sexualized by the male gaze. While this is also fitting as an example of External Influence (to be discussed in Chapter 6), it is significant to note here for its specific influence on how some femme individuals see their own erotic selves. Several women of varying ages expressed challenges with sexualization, including Alicia, a New York heterosexual woman in her mid-30s. In Alicia's particular case, constant experiences of objectification encountered in her environment put her in a position where, as she noted, "I don't think I really . . . see [myself as] sexiness." She clarified by adding,

> I don't know if I want to use people on the street to describe it, because, uh, I feel like a lot of times when men are on the street, I just feel like they reduce me to ass. So I don't know that . . . ugh, hrmm . . .

Throughout our conversation, Alicia's ability to conceptualize her Erotic Self on her own appeared to be hampered by automatic acquiescence to her external experiences with others—a deference arguably informed by living life, again, under that particular gaze.

To summarize, Magnets and Product coders prioritize attraction as a primary dynamic in establishing the Erotic Self. In addition, and perhaps even more than others, both Magnets and Products may experience external challenges in defining one's self along the way. While African American male-identified individuals may have unique contexts in which their Magnet personalities grow and develop, Black femmes appear to have a potentially harder time expressing Magnet personalities and contending with the pressures of undesired Product assignment. Femme-identified folks who are aware of or relate to a Magnet personality in particular may feel conflicted about prioritizing the attractions of others if they have previous negative thoughts about how they view such attractions, are not successful in attracting what they wish or receive attraction in particularly toxic ways. The male gaze may ultimately serve to distort femme individuals' relationships with their own erotic selves, hindering their ability to define and exude them authentically.

Sexual Brand

Sexual identity does not, by and large, explain who an Erotic Self is, but rather suggests how it might want to be imagined by an observer. In other words, it is their *Sexual Brand*, the term I have selected for this category. Sexual identity did not emerge as a constitutive aspect of sexiness among the sample. Indeed, at no point in this study, either generally or specifically, were sexual identities or sexual identity labels mentioned as part of the eight sexiness channels. That said, what was clear among many respondents was that one's identity does matter, particularly when considering or discussing significant aspects of one's larger erotic universe. Saucy Teal in Atlanta provided a solid opening definition of *Sexual Brand*: "a descriptor or a very generic term that may describe someone's [sexual] preference, how they want to be handled . . ." While it does not usually speak to an entity's essence or essential characteristics, one's Sexual Brand does provide a gateway for helping others better understand the Erotic Self in question—its relationships, erotic motivations/attractions and, perhaps, politics.

A Sexual Brand can be a clear communicative tool for the individual, helping to facilitate negotiation of desired sensory experiences and opening up avenues for articulating how that individual organizes, or wishes to organize, their sexual life and relationships. When discussing sexuality in general, sexual orientations were the types of brands most often mentioned by respondents (e.g., "queer," "gay," "heterosexual"). Gender/gender expression (e.g., "male," "woman," "genderqueer"), erotic communities (e.g., "kink," "BDSM," "poly") and race were mentioned as well.

Sexual Brand was not a term used by respondents in this sample; however, *sexual identity*—the concept from which it derives—did emerge as a salient concept among individuals seemingly better versed in the overall subject of sexuality. Lelah, a Virginia student affairs professional in her early 30s, described her awareness of Sexual Branding as an emergent result of interacting with LGBTQ students at the local university where she works. As she specifically noted, "[I]n the work that I do, when people use sexuality it's oftentimes in terms of, um, how someone identifies." Victoria, a paraprofessional at Planned Parenthood, also described her understanding of sexuality as being informed and enhanced by her professional experience:

> Victoria: In my professional life, because of where I work, I don't even bring my personal sexuality into the thought, I guess? . . . I don't kinda think about me and my sexual preferences or about me being sexual until that [after work] "switch" hits.
>
> Me: So it sounds like from a professional perspective, sexuality is more about sexual orientation, gender identity and those sorts of things, whereas in your own life it's like, it's this experience of, like, being with each other, enjoying each other, that sort of thing.
>
> Victoria: Yes [*nods*].

For these individuals in particular, Sexual Branding served as a key factor in differentiating sexiness from sexuality given its conversational prevalence in their respective professional spaces.

Jasmine in Brooklyn (discussed earlier as a "Relator") spoke more explicitly about how sexual branding overruns discussions of sexuality within their professional spaces:

> [m]y first thought when someone's like, "What do you think about sexuality?" I think—the first thing I would think is an identity—is "What is your identity?" I think that some—oftentimes that's another way for folks to ask that question? And then, just in the spaces that I'm in, I think that's what people are referring to. So when I think about the word *sexuality*—when that is asked to me—that's what I'm thinking about, is identity. Not necessarily what makes me feel good—but with the training that I have, I understand that that word is so much more than identity.

Given the circles Lelah, Victoria and Jasmine find themselves in by virtue of their professional lives, it follows that their consideration of sexuality might be more nuanced in this way. In all three cases, the label of "sexuality professional" could be said to also play a part in their Sexual Brand, as all of them (as well as several others in this study) expressed some mindfulness about the ways in which their professional perspective could be juxtaposed with their personal sexual ideation.

Several younger respondents in the sample also seemed particularly interested in the ways that Sexual Brand at least informed their conceptualizations of sexiness. Jai and King, both individuals in their early 20s living in the Midwest, spoke to their experiences of being pansexual. Though Jai expressed some trepidation in owning her Sexual Brand, she was clear that doing so meant being able to "fit the *mold I've created of what sexiness is*" (italics mine). King, who seemed perhaps more comfortable in their brand, remarked,

> I don't care what anyone has in their pants, as long as they, you know, are open to me. And, um, that's what matters to me the most. I don't care what you look like or anything. Don't care what you identify as. I respect it, as long as people respect me.

In King's case, the Sexual Brand of "pansexual" helped them successfully articulate a sexual philosophy of openness with respect to gender and orientation.

Though not as young as the others, Lelah shared a personal story of her own about how Sexual Brand shapes, and can be shaped by, one's sexiness development:

> [s]o when I came out . . . I came out as a lesbian. And so I only really was attracted to and dated cisgender women. And then I met my current partner, who's amazing, um, and had just transitioned [to a transmasculine identity]. And so I had to have this conversation with myself, almost "What does this mean?" So body and, like, spirit were not aligning in what I thought my reality was. And I didn't care. And so, then, what does it mean that I am a lesbian and this person reads to the world as a man? Um . . . yeah . . . so I then because of that . . . now I think I operate in the world in terms of sex and sexuality as more of a spirit connection: if I vibe with you, then I'm gonna wanna have sex with you, rather than what's between your legs and what I conceptualize gender to be . . . so I kinda operate without gender at this point.

In Lelah's case, the changing Sexual Brand exhibited through her partner's gender affirmation fostered a shift in Lelah's sexiness development that increased her reliance on the Erotic Energy sexiness channel. While she continues to use branding to effectively communicate with new significant others in her primary relationship (both are polyamorous), Lelah is clear that the labels she and her partner use are less about sexual definition than about sexual self-description.

To reiterate, then, the Sexual Brand does not adequately encapsulate sexiness or even explain the full erotic universe that is Sexuality. That said, it is an often utilized tool that can be effective in the navigation of sexuality and sexiness development, particularly in how one's Erotic Self is presented or explained to others. In fact, no persona of the Erotic Self explains sexiness more than it characterizes the person with chief responsibility for determining how their sexiness development ultimately proceeds. Thus concludes this chapter on the Erotic Self and the six emergent Erotic Self personas found among this sample. We proceed in the next chapter to the final operating element within the BSE model, that of External Influences.

Note

[1] Anecdotes among researchers and other sexuality practitioners with whom I've shared this work thus far suggest that the Erotic Self is a salient enough concept that further research into its potential dimensions and elements may indeed be warranted.

6

EXTERNAL INFLUENCES

SYLVIA'S STORY

Sylvia is a 67-year-old woman who lives in Omaha, Nebraska. Born and raised in that general area, she is a pillar of her community, having a strong influence on everyone around her, children and adults alike. Sylvia has seen a lot in her community and lifetime, including the direct effects of Jim Crow on her family as well as those of the crack epidemic on her neighborhood. In fact, part of how Sylvia's family ended up in Omaha is due to her father's running away from his Texas hometown in the early '40s after mobs threatened to lynch him over the false belief that he'd raped a white girl he was having consensual sex with (at the time they were both 17 years old). He escaped to the U.S. Army for a short stint using fabricated paperwork and then eventually married Sylvia's mother before settling down in the mostly Black north side of the city. Sylvia's brother Carmichael would become a community leader in his own right, opening the first community center for young people, where he taught boys and girls alike how to box and play basketball and encouraged them to stay away from gangs and the drug trade of the '80s and '90s.

Sylvia's daughter Angel was 37 when she revealed to Sylvia that she had been molested by Carmichael in her early teens. The news rocked Sylvia's world, as while she knew Angel had several social and emotional challenges growing up, she never thought that her brother would be related to any of them. As Angel relayed her story, Sylvia remembered something she once overheard Carmichael say about Angel after she began pubertal development at age 12: "they gon' need to put that girl on a leash; she about to become a stallion, that one!" Besides urging Angel to cover up more around men since she was "becoming a woman," Sylvia didn't address the matter further, thinking she had already done enough and that she "didn't want to put any more ideas in Angel's head than were necessary." It was Carmichael's recent and unexpected death that prompted Angel's revelation. Because his death came as a surprise to the entire city, Sylvia's suggestion to Angel was that she avoid telling anyone else about her experience, saying, "It happened so long ago and he's dead now. Wouldn't make sense to ruin another Black man's reputation." Sylvia and Angel still speak and visit with each other; however, their relationship has been strained considerably since then.

Sylvia has never been married and lost Angel's father to gun violence when Angel was nine years old. While she has had occasional lovers since that time, her belief at this point in her life is that "it'll probably end up being me and Jesus from here on out."

Now that I have discussed the nine most fundamental aspects of Black Sexual Epistemology (Eight Channels of Sexiness and The Erotic Self), I would like to use this chapter to cover aspects of the model shared by the sample that were not inherent to sexiness but were significant factors nonetheless. I coded these particular elements using the category "External Influences." The experiences in this category do not explain sexuality and sexiness in and of themselves, though they may explain alterations in how an individual conceptualizes or experiences them. In an ideal world, Erotic Selves successfully navigate their sexuality by defining, cultivating and living out exuded being and sensory experience in the precise ways they intend. In the real world, however, external influences both amplify and frustrate sexiness development, affecting the quality and quantity of one's experience.

From the engineering perspective, external influences can be best understood as "gain," which is responsible for moderating the frequency of sexiness an erotic being emits—specifically the strength of one's transmitting signal. When gain levels are balanced, the signals emitted by the erotic being are clearly reflected in the channels they are funneled through. The Erotic Self can be sure this is happening when it feels the least dissonance in the sexiness it is exuding or experiencing. The hyper-experience of external influence, however, can cause gains in increases or decreases, resulting in hyper-amped emission and distorted sound if too much and compromised emission and weak sound if too low. An Erotic Self may recognize this is happening when, for example, it attempts to raise the level of a certain channel of its control panel and does not get the desired effect. In this case, there is an external influence that is serving to limit what that erotic being is capable of emitting, either in that moment or for a particular period of time. That said, external influences can also be positive, helping to right gain levels that have been distorted by previous adverse experiences or even misperceptions enacted by the Erotic Self. In this way, external influences serve to both balance gain and put it out of balance, making gain change able to be positive, negative or neutral in nature.

External Influences can emerge from a wide range of source types, including cultural, political, interpersonal and intrapsychic. The following list does not represent the conclusive universe of influential factors. The actual list may expand as much as the number of erotic selves on the planet and ultimately falls outside the parameters of this book. Summaries of various types of external factors raised by individuals within this sample, however, are briefly described in the following sections.

Racial Maligning

As was explained at the beginning of this book, understanding the role of race in African American sexuality was a chief aim of my original research. While the conversations I had with some respondents did reveal aspects of sexiness informing the category of Performative Blackness, the vast majority of respondents expressed that race ("being Black") had a negative effect on their understanding of sexuality, so much so that after about 20 conversations, I had to explicitly ask if race had any positive effects that were not immediately considered. The general consensus among the sample, however, was that racial maligning created a weakening effect on individuals' sexiness volume and development. This dynamic was most commonly described as being a "Box," a restrictive experience in which acceptable forms of sexual expression—non-kinky, demure, heterosexual monogamy, for example—are allowed but from which expressions that do not fit traditional (or perceivably traditional) social norms are excluded. Ashton, a bisexual Baltimore woman in her early 30s, provided a quintessential description of The Box during our conversation:

> [s]o I think . . . The Box is just "the man," "the woman." It is the man going to work. It is the man, uh, providing for the family. It is the, the woman at home, cooking, cleaning, you know, maintaining life. It is just man/woman, you know, you have your two kids, you guys go to church—it is just that . . . typical, you know, "family." It's, it is what—they put us in a box. It is what that's supposed to look like. And if it's not that, no one understands it: "[w]hat is that? How is that? How can you be managed?" You know what I mean? Questions come about if you look like anything outside of The Box.

According to other responses, The Box can include a number of other attitudes and behaviors, including expressed resistance to particular sexual proclivities or to sex positivity as a whole. Several folks—particularly femme and queer respondents—cited The Box as a challenge not only for themselves in being able to fully access sexiness but also for the entire Black community, limiting the freedom with which sexuality can be discussed and negotiated:

> [t]o me, The Box is scary. . . . I don't see how anyone could be happy in that box because it's like, you're not opening your mind to all the possibilities of who you can love and who can love you . . . and, you know, we kinda force ourselves to think certain ways, and it's kinda hard to unlearn those things . . .
>
> (King)

> I have had to overcome a lot of things . . . talking about sexuality. I mean, first of all, I was raised by a Caribbean mother, um, so I will say a West Indian household. So there were just certain things that you just didn't talk about . . . and it was kind of hard in the beginning because, you know, first of all, although I was always encouraged to speak my mind, when it came to sex, the attitude I was reared with was "Well, it's something you do in the dark. It's something that you don't really talk

about" . . . it just was not done. . . . So when I got this [sexual] homework assignment from my friend, it forced me to think about it, and sex, in a different kind of way. . . . He said to me, "What turns you on? You know, what's your fantasy? What do you love to do?" . . . I *know* that I was embarrassed to just put it into words. I was embarrassed to talk about fantasies. You know, I was embarrassed to talk about sexuality.

(Alex)

Like, I feel like [Baby Boomers are] a lot more concerned about what white people think and, like, being more respectable—like respectability politics—like, they care so much about how we're perceived when we do certain things, like can't be too loud, can't dress this way, can't walk this way, can't go to these places or whatever . . . so I think that even down to sex we're, like, afraid to experiment or be, like, openly sexual because it would be seen as [disrespectable]. It would be seen as perpetuating stereotypes that we're trying to, like, skirt.

(Jai)

Many aspects of The Box dovetail with individuals' conceptualizations of religion and its influence on Black sexuality. Gender and sexuality expectations enforced by traditional religion appear to find their way into individuals' conceptualizations of Blackness, in that perceptions of religion's influence are deemed to be inherent to Black culture and Black life. As Ashton also shared in our discussion:

> I think that religion is the cornerstone of our community. I think that you . . . the church is just such an important piece of our community, so I think it always, in some way, shape, form or fashion, plays into everything we do as a community. To whether we think something is positive or negative, whether we do something or don't do something, whether we get up on Sunday and go to church or don't go to church. Whether, you know, we have a bad day and it's, like, "Lord, what's going on!" Like, you speak to God this day because you're having a *good* day; you speak to God because you're having a *bad* day. I think it all, I think it all revolves around the church. It's always been a cornerstone of our community.

Religion was cited as the second largest influence on the creation and maintenance of The Box after Whiteness/White supremacy. Given the ways that religion—and Western Christianity in particular—was used historically for transmitting racialized sexual norms among African American people, this conflation of ideologies makes sense.

Several respondents also shared stories from relationships and other everyday encounters highlighting the race-based dynamics operating within them. Among these included fetishization ("While I was looking past race, they were enamored with my race in a way I thought we weren't doing"; "I dated white girls 'cause I could"), racial stereotyping ("I felt very threatened by Black male sexuality"), racialized double standards ("Expectations made of me were definitely different than expectations made of my white counterparts"), body shaming ("I had a lot of body image issues about the distribution of my weight"), marginalization ("I wasn't good enough to date but good enough to fuck") and general hypersexual idealizing ("There's the whole 'Black people with vaginas have better vaginas'"; "It's always sorta been this social experiment"). In addition, participants appeared to have a keen awareness of certain ways White supremacy affects social norms around attractiveness and desirability. Crystal, a 40-plus dark-skinned woman in Chicago, shared an example of how White supremacist dynamics informed her self-image through interpersonal experiences of colorism:

> [y]ou kinda feel—like, I mean, you're definitely aware that you are different. You're not like the other girls. You're not blond-haired, you're not blue-eyed, you're not light-skinned—that was also sort of—that also sort of, um . . . influenced my perception of myself because growing up you kinda knew the dudes in your neighborhood went for a very specific type of girl. And that, you know, hasn't really changed much within the last 30 years. So you always sorta feel like you're not, you know, you're not the ideal. And that's reinforced by everything you see; every piece of media you see reinforces that idea.

Applying BSE to this example, it appears that macro-level social norms about skin color dampened the gain volume of Crystal's comportment channel frequency, causing her over time to question her control panel's sexiness volume capacity.

In almost all examples raised among the sample, experiences of racial maligning were externally imposed, extending from how participants were viewed or treated by others and not necessarily how they first viewed or treated themselves. As another example, external perceptions of Yoncé's biracial identity resulted in imposed assumptions about her sexual experience and prowess:

> [b]ecause I was, like, this exotic person, I was expected to perform as such. And really, I wasn't that sexual in high school at all. And I think, you know, when I would talk to my dad, not necessarily about sex, but about the fact that I felt like nobody wanted to date me, he was like, "[Yoncé], they don't know what to do with you."

In this particular case, Yoncé experienced a direct maligning of her Performative Blackness volume input by others in her environment. Instead of affirming her erotic being's authentic input, her peers and friends applied unnecessary gain via stereotypical assumptions about Yonce's racial identity, such that her sexiness frequency in that particular channel became perceived as being stronger than it was actually intended to be.

A commonly reported response by the participants to the external influence of racial maligning was to actively resist gain-shifting efforts by either physically distancing themselves from the individuals they were involved with or training their minds to resist the particular messaging they were receiving about their sexual selves. Jewel in Atlanta discussed such resistance in her own sexiness development journey by stressing that, with regard to her aesthetic attraction template,

> Tall and curvy are what I like, but I also think that is a part of this radicalization that continues to happen as I get older, which is that it's not what society . . . says [sexiness is] to be . . . that reverberates in my life, in the sense of the deprogramming of myself in really being an actor in White supremacy and anti-Blackness . . .

Leslie in Maryland displayed similar resistance in noting that

> I think someone can be sexy without being conventionally attractive. . . . I think that's also important, too, especially as someone who is not considered conventionally attractive by, like, European beauty standards. . . . I can still be sexy [*laughs*], you know? Even if there are people who may not think that I'm pretty.

In both cases, these individuals began to rebalance the adverse external influence of racial maligning by actively growing more in tune with their own needs and with counter-narratives that push back against the racist norm.

Commercialism

Race and economics appear to be the most cited external influences on sexuality among this sample. Regarding the latter, several respondents were quick to point out the role of the marketplace in establishing both a foundation of what sexiness is and means and what specific people, places and things fit within the category of sexual attractiveness. Nickie, discussed in Chapter 4 for her love of Valentine's Day and chocolate, believes firmly in the influence of commercialism on general conceptualizations of sexiness, so much so that she considers them nearly inextricable:

> Me: Thinking about the market, is it possible in your mind to imagine what, if the market were removed, if that would change your idea of what is sexy or sexiness?
>
> Nickie: I don't believe so. I mean, because I feel like these types of things we're inundated with as very, very, very young children, and so we're essentially programmed to think, you know, "red is a sexy color" and then "black is a sexy color" ... but I guess it's just because of the marketing ... if you took the marketing away, I don't think [red] would still be as sexy.
>
> Me: Okay, so then let's imagine that. If there were no marketing, what, what do you think sexiness would be to you?
>
> Nickie: [ponders] It still goes back—I feel like it still goes back to the marketing. 'Cause, I mean, I think beaches are sexy, if we're gonna take out, like, colors. But, water ... I mean, those things exist without the market, but still, the market uses them to promote sexiness. I know especially like [indecipherable] commercials, it's always a couple walking along the beach and sitting in a hammock on the beach—that's part of the marketing, you know? That's ... sexy.

From this perspective, sexiness is a commodity that can be used to procure financial resources for those capable of skillfully marketing it. Deeper than this, however, commercialism not only reinforces exuded beings and sensual activities that individuals may already have preexisting schema for (walking along the beach) but also has the power to preset the signal strength of sexiness for new inputs for which individuals have no original frame of reference (e.g., red as a sexy color). Given its social power and ubiquity, the marketplace appears to make it quite difficult for some individuals to focus their attention on personal estimations of sexiness, particularly if what is personally attractive does not fit mainstream ideals.

Like racial maligning, resistance to commercialism appeared common within the sample as well, with several respondents highlighting specific ways they'd attempted to rebalance the influence of mainstream notions of sexiness in their lives, even exhibiting examples of said behavior during our conversation. Alaia in North Carolina, who originally wrote "Vickie's" (Victoria's Secret) on her sexiness primer sheet, found herself changing her mind upon reflection, concluding that such imagery represents "how the media would define sexiness instead of how I would define sexiness." She went on to explain that "after I wrote 'Vickie's' it wasn't gonna be true to who I was and what I felt sexiness was." Ava, a heterosexual Philadelphia woman in her late 20s, discussed rebalancing corporeality volume input, in particular by noting the following about print media:

> if I think about, like, magazines and stuff, like, sex sells, but to me that presentation is very forced. It's like, "Here's a boob; that's sexiness"—which could be, of course—but I'm just thinking about what I would find attractive [which] is someone just not trying too hard.

Aaron, who has been discussed at several earlier points throughout this book, reported going even further to rebalance commercial influence on their comportment volume input by asserting a norm in which

> I don't really follow the rules. And part of it is because . . . I don't want to make it too easy to find me attractive. Because I feel like people put too much into that. . . . I've stopped caring. I've stopped really putting a lot of effort in, and the people that are around for that get preference.

To a large degree, then, while the marketplace does directly influence what individuals have access to in the mainstream for conceptualizing sexiness, it does not serve as the automatic final authority for what is eventually integrated into an individual's psyche.

Chronic Pain, Illness and Disability

There are external influences that are social in nature, and then there are those that are medical or related to forces outside a social arena. As much as one may desire to achieve a certain channel output, challenges in one's physical being may frustrate the quality of one's exudation or sensory experience volume input. Chronic pain, illness and disability were the types of medical influences reported in this sample and refer to any type of perceived physical or physiological challenges a person may experience in their body. When encountered, they appear to directly affect one's exudation and sensory strength. For example, Cornell, a heterosexual married man in Maryland, explained how having been born with a spinal deformity has, on occasion, affected his Comportment input volume:

> [w]hen I wasn't actively taking [male enhancement pills] and wasn't— you know, either feeling exhausted from the day, or my partner saying, "Well, you know, I don't know if . . . you're attracted to me because you're not . . . aroused when I'm ready for sex . . ." it obviously isn't [that he's not attracted], but . . . because, I guess, the way that birth defect affects the spinal cord, and especially the lower part of the spinal cord, it just screws things up and doesn't allow for full arousal that you would expect during the course of [sexual intercourse].

Olive, a Philadelphia woman in her early 40s, expressed similar sentiments about her experience with chronic pain:

> I have rheumatoid arthritis. So when I'm in pain it's just like, "Oh my God." Like, I don't feel . . . like, I just don't feel confident in myself in general. So then, when you're talking about adding, like, a sexuality or sexiness component to it, it's like a "uh, no." So then most days that's not the case, but like, when I'm really not, like, feeling well it's like I'm just not really feeling myself overall.

Stories like Olive's were reported by Valentina in Washington, D.C., and Nina in Philadelphia. Betty in Kentucky discussed life experience with chronic pain that included additional implications:

> [i]f I have a migraine, sex is completely off the table. Don't fucking touch me; turn the lights off, get out. I don't want to hear you *breathing*. And I've had partners who just don't get it. They like, "Oh, you just

don't wanna have sex or you have a headache," and I'm like, "No . . . that's not how that works."

Betty and Cornell appeared to share the experience of their disability having bi-directional adverse influence, as both reported partners who internalized their disability as being a disruption to the gain levels in their Relationship and Erotic Energy channels as well.

Like racial maligning and commercialism, experiences of chronic pain, illness or disability do not translate into permanent, or even automatic, signal imbalance. Cornell noted that, for him, "[t]here are times when I'm at my highest and I feel sexy, and then there are times when I feel really low, and I don't say it because rather than saying it, I just work on it." Though he did not elaborate with detail, Cornell's employment of gain rebalancing strategies provides additional evidence of the individual's capacity to work at signal strength even if it appears curtailed in a particularly daunting way.

Sexual Trauma

A small number of individuals within the sample reported histories of sexual trauma in the form of assault, abuse and "misuse" (Brant & Tisza, 1977). These included encounters experienced in both childhood and adulthood and were explicitly coded as problematic experiences by the reporting individuals. Though involving inherently sexual encounters, experiences of abuse, assault and the like are not sexiness. Instead, they affect the gain applied to both one's sexiness signal input and one's subsequent exudation or sensory volume. Additionally, these experiences can have a direct influence on perceptions of safety, morality, consent and sensual pleasure. On a macro-level, ideas around sexual trauma merged with race and gender for several participants. In Ginger Dee's estimation, historical treatment of Black bodies through slave rape and media hyper-sexualization established an intra-cultural precedent for neglecting the reported sexual trauma of Black women in the present:

> I feel like in our culture, we more so hide family issues and problems as to not out a perpetrator, essentially, right? So incest and rape, in many instances—I feel like in many ways, too, because Black women are over-sexualized, when we become victims of rape, we're asked—we're blamed and made to take the onus for someone victimizing us.

Though she was clear that the sexualized remnants of slavery were not limited in effect to women, Ginger's assertion was that Black women's experiences with this history warranted more nuanced consideration.

It was women who reported experiencing sexual misuse in this sample, although despite the history Ginger raises, most cases occurred intraracially. Lola reported such a story when I asked her about the quality of sexual experiences she had had with other Black people: "I, uh, unfortunately, was sexually assaulted by a [Black man], so I'm having a really hard time looking past that one particular incident. . . . That didn't go very well." While she did not see this experience as capable of having a long-term effect on future experiences with Black men, her encounter was recent and significant enough to our conversation to limit the degree of sensory input she desired with them in the immediate moment. Experiences of sexual trauma can erect difficult boundaries for individuals to surpass in being able to build and maintain strong sensory experiences with both others and the self. Evelyn, a queer femme in Washington, D.C., shared such a story related to her sense of comportment:

> [i]t's taken me a while to be confident in myself because, growing up, there were certain expectations. . . . For me, it was me being separate from my body, where I always considered my body kind of, like, a joke.

Dissociation, in Evelyn's case, had direct consequences not only on the input levels of her erotic volume but also on her capacity to access the channels themselves. As she asserted, "[W]hen someone is violated at that point, um, you kinda feel separate from it."

Betty, who was assaulted by a Black man as a child, also reported not experiencing long-term adverse impressions of Black men due to her experiences; indeed, she was one of the most notable proponents of male Performative Blackness discussed in Chapter 3. Her experience did, however, highly inform her impressions of consent within the sexual encounter. In particular, consent was noted as an additional sign of sexiness for Betty. She added during our conversation that

> I can be aroused by someone who I think I have a connection with, but before any touching takes place, anything like that, I need—it's *really* important for me—to have consent to do that and for them to have consent to touch me.

The lack of consent Betty experienced during her sexual assault placed the imperative to command it at all points of her adult sexual encounters, tying directly into the quality of her sensual pleasure experiences today:

> [f]or me, consent is freedom . . . although I have been in relationships and been in situations where, um, someone has done something sexually without having that conversation prior to and I still enjoyed it, right? And still allowed it to happen, allowed it to continue, but having the "Before the Pants Come Off" talk, as I call it, still allows me more freedom, which then ties into more pleasure.

Betty went on to explain how her assault has resulted in physiological challenges to both her exudation and sensory input volume in adulthood, providing particular detail regarding how much more tense her body feels in situations when explicit consent has not been negotiated. However, through active and intentional negotiation before each new encounter, Betty has been able to rebalance her signal gain in such a way as to mitigate what her initial assault experience distorted.

As a final point, it is important to note that stories reported from the sample may not represent the total universe of sexually traumatic experiences that exist. Particularly given that I did not explicitly ask about the topic, it may follow that some within the sample chose not to volunteer otherwise pertinent or effectual information in this regard. Silence around disclosure of sexual trauma and misuse may represent its own form of external influence, linked to presently undetermined sexiness frequency effects. Further examination of this dynamic falls outside the parameters of the present research.

Sexual Precocity

Most sexology professionals would not code child sexuality as being problematic in and of itself; however, a particular reported instance of childhood sexual development emerged as being significant enough to warrant being coded at this level. At the end of each formal interview, participants were invited to share additional information that was not previously solicited. During this portion of our conversation, Diamond, a Southern New Jersey preacher's wife in her late 30s, chose to share pieces of her family history that involved a number of early sexual experiences, including pornography exposure, intra-familial sexual encounters, teen pregnancy, loss of a relative due to sexual violence and early sexual debut. Though the experiences she described appear on par with those reported by adult samples more broadly (Martinson, 1994), Diamond noted that, for her,

> processing [my history] . . . I felt as though I was open to a lot more and, uh . . . sexually vulnerable? . . . I felt like, at the time, the only thing that I really did get feeling from was sexual encounters. And I think it was because I was exposed to so much already. . . . I think it just all stems back to early exposure.

Indeed, even though Diamond attributed her early childhood sexual history to the sexual confidence she exudes within her current sex life, her use of the term *vulnerable* and assertion of numbness related to noncoital sensory experience are evidence that she does not see this connection positively and that she may have some feelings of conflict about how this informs volume input for her control panel.

As somewhat of a religious leader in her present life, Diamond noted an additional challenge in reconciling her more strict Christian faith with the sense of sexual confidence she gained from her upbringing, especially that related to same-gender sexual attraction. She noted that

> [w]hen I think back to my upbringing and my religious belief, um, yeah, it *can* be a conflict, but because of—because I do still believe in this [Christian] way of life, I'm gonna continue to fight every day to be as best the person that I am, knowing that I will never be perfect, but it's still something that I try to line up with.

Because of the ways that Christian conservatism is often linked to sexual limitation, Diamond's present religious beliefs may add an extra layer of judgment onto her childhood sexual experiences, leading her to possibly see them as responsible for her present internal struggle. On another note, Diamond's present-day views also raise a question about their potential relationship to racial maligning via the ideology of The Box discussed earlier. During our conversation, Diamond noted that "I don't think my sex and sexuality is [sic] a problem *now* because there are so many ways I think I have and I *can* explore my sexuality with my spouse and still be fulfilled in that area." At the same time, she was clear that despite the variety of avenues she pursued as a result of her sexual history and the sense of sexual confidence she reported gaining from it, it was both important and sufficient to her to curtail the strength of what those experiences signaled in her to focus solely on what would fall within her heterosexual marriage and the sanctioned boundaries of her faith. Diamond did not implicate race in her analysis, so the question of explicit racial maligning in this case remains unclear. In fact, what may be more salient here is The Box emerging as an affirming element of Diamond's sexiness at this point in her development trajectory, appearing as a desired readjustment of old, distorted sexiness experienced through her childhood.

Technology

A discussion of external influences on sexiness would be incomplete without consideration of the role played in establishing the parameters of sexual ideation. Many respondents in the sample reported that their first encounters with sex occurred through watching media like music videos, social media sites and internet pornography. Much like commercialism, advancements in internet technology have come to greatly influence what consumers have access to for their personal edification. Michelle, a queer 20-something woman in Rhode Island, shared a story from her experience with internet porn that speaks to both its standalone influence and intersection with racial maligning:

> I think when I think of sexuality, I think of bodies and, like, porn. And that's not something I like to think about; it's something I think about automatically because that's how I was introduced to sex.... I remember watching porn as a child and, like, watching lesbian porn ... and I saw all these, like, thin White women ... with long straight hair, and I was, like, a fat Black kid with, like, braids [*laughs*]. And I was like, "This isn't necessarily me that I'm seeing." So now when I look at porn I try to, like, find Black women, but everything I see with Black women is like, "Ebony Bitch Gets Fucked by White Dick," and, like, I don't really like this way of othering Black women or, like, making them into, like, ratchet ... that doesn't interest me.

Michelle went on to lament the lack of race and body diversity in sexual media and its influence on her self-image ("the black figures I've seen have been thinner Black women with straight hair, and I haven't seen myself as a fat Black woman with kinky hair in sexuality") while also citing individuals like Lizzo for single-handedly offering possibility models for women like herself to reimagine the exudation and sensory signal strength that are resonant and accessible to them. On one level, the vastness of the internet has opened innumerable doors for individuals seeking sexual entertainment that extends beyond what might be available to them in (or what has been sanctioned by) their offline environment; however, when driven by the desires of particularly lucrative yet racist markets, people at the racial margins (including the intersections thereof) may still face limitations finding avenues through which to comfortably come into their own sense of personal sexiness, particularly if they attempt to do so by recalibrating the images and experiences they've always been offered.

Technology links directly with commercialism via the perpetually growing number of avenues through which revenue-generating media can be directed. Additionally, evolutions in the processing and transmission of internet data may also connect to what one learns to identify as sexiness, along with the sensual activities one believes to be at one's disposal. Cornell in Maryland, discussed earlier in the chapter, raised an interesting point about this fact, alluding to how it may be happening even when the process is not entirely deliberate:

> [s]exiness is different for everybody, and I think we've done a terrible job as a culture . . . as far as not understanding what sexy actually is and just kinda leaving it up to math to decide for us when we search for it on the internet . . . because the world as it stands now, what is considered sexy is—I mean, you could type it in, and it's literally whatever Google Images finds, right? And that's literally an algorithm—there aren't people on the other end saying, "This is sexy, this is sexy, this is sexy," so . . . it's literally a range of things for a range of tastes.

Time will tell what present shifts in technology will influence the sexiness signal inputs of the future, particularly with the steady and growing reliance on virtual platforms for most human interactions (e.g., online/virtual dating, OnlyFans); that said, it is clear they have a significant relationship to many of the sexiness experiences individuals have in the present day.

Professional Identity

Finally, it is significant that this sample included a number of sex educators and other sexuality practitioners, as this professional identity directly affected the ways that several of them viewed both their erotic selves and sexuality as a whole. Individuals that have been formally trained to transmit any level of information to a larger audience are usually first indoctrinated into a particular body of "common" knowledge as well as in a particular ethos for thinking about it. If the subject matter in question directly relates to subjects within the individual's personal life, as sexuality education often does, this information will likely influence how that professional integrates that information. Jasmine in Brooklyn, discussed earlier, was one such individual for whom the birth of their professional identity resulted in a dislodging of previously established sexual ideas and norms. When I met with them and their partner, George, the following exchange took place after a question I asked about the nature of sexuality:

> Jasmine: I feel like my professional self has taken over, um, I think I have to think about . . . I have to go back to, like, the original thought before I intellectualize it. So I have to stop the professor in me and then go back to "Okay, what was the first thought you had?"
>
> George: Primal.
>
> Jasmine: Primal, yes, the lizard brain, the primal answering of that question.

During the question asking about the thoughts that came to one's mind when thinking of sexuality as a concept, Jasmine found themself relying on their professional training to answer with the response of sexual orientation, when their "lizard brain," as they described it, was inclined to think of porn, representing their own prior personal experience with the notion.

Cleopatra, a 20-something educator in North Carolina, cited Dailey's five circles as her answer to the same question and asserted that while they did not likely cover all the conceptual bases of sexuality existing on Earth, nor actually represented the answer she would have given as her noneducator self, they were sufficient as "a baseline" for establishing common norms for general audiences to build on. In fact, when I asked her how much of her own particular sexuality was considered or practiced through her professional lens, her response was, "It's not . . . I would say it's not." Victoria in Buffalo, New York, was another practitioner who practiced this sort of compartmentalization between her professional and personal self, with its also affecting how she understood sexuality in her personal versus professional life. She appeared to express no challenges with the seeming disconnect, however, noting that

> [i]t works for me. Because I am an individual where I, kind of, separate, you know, I have my world life here, I have a personal life at home here, maybe family and friends and things over here—I kinda don't combine everything, because that's just my preference. So, you know, I don't mind coming to work and working on what we work on here . . . and then when I go home, that's a completely different world.

While Jasmine, Cleopatra and Victoria experienced personal–professional separation in their approaches to sexuality, Betty in Kentucky experienced what appears to be the opposite relationship between identities, establishing an emergent identity of herself as a "sexiness promoter" in both areas of her life. Specifically, she asserted, "I see myself promoting [sexiness] . . . as a sexual person and as a sexuality educator." I probed further and received the following explanation:

> [f]or me, it's kinda like [sexiness] are [sic] the things, through my experience . . . that I want, that I desire, that I see other people want and desire and don't know how to ask or don't know that there's a connection between these things and their own personal sexuality.

> Me: In what ways, if at all, does your experience now as a sex educator affect your current sexuality experience?

> Betty: Um, I think they're so intertwined because even as an adult I *still* have so many questions. Um, I thought that I was the liberal sexologist, by self-disclaimer, until [beginning formal graduate sexology training]. And it was so many other things that were impactful that I didn't know anything about—like I knew them, but I didn't know them, or I knew them but didn't know the name for them. . . . That's something I see, and so it's something that I teach.

As can be seen, then, while the effect is different among practitioners depending on their particular frame of reference and relationship to the work, there is a process that occurs in navigating the relationship between the professional and personal sexual selves that is directly influenced by the establishment of the former in human sexuality. A curious question for future research in this area may be the degree to which professional identity as a sexuality practitioner increases an individual's capacity to see and assert control over their gain management, particularly if their particular work in the field focuses on issues and topics that overlap their personal lived experience in the way Betty's does.

BSE Model Summary

To summarize, Black Sexual Epistemology is a framework that attempts to explain the lived experience of sexuality among a sample of African American people. It begins with a conceptualization of Sexiness, which includes eight various Channels or manifestations of Exuded Being and Sensory Experience. Exuded Being can be best understood as the embodied quality of erotic energy, while Sensory Experience includes the body of activities/events through which Exuded Being is encountered. The Eight Channels of Sexiness are Comportment, Corporeality, Erotic Energy, Performative Blackness, Sensual Pleasure, Mental Excitation, Relationship and Positive Affect.

Comportment, Corporeality, Erotic Energy and Performative Blackness are the four channels of sexiness under the label Exuded Being. Comportment generally refers to the ways in which an individual carries themselves and includes the sub-themes of confidence, competence, compassion and self-sovereignty. Corporeality refers to the attractive nature of bodies and inanimate objects. Erotic Energy describes the palpable advent of physiological energy felt between and among individuals and includes attraction, fluidity, depth, power and "the unknowable." Performative Blackness speaks specifically about ways that elements of Comportment and Corporeality intersect with race-based cultural expression.

Sensual Pleasure, Mental Excitation, Relationship and Positive Affect are the four channels of Sensory Experience. Sensual Pleasure highlights activities that engage the five main senses: sight, sound, smell, taste and touch. Mental Excitation speaks to arousal stimulated by mental engagement, including intelligence and fantasy. Connection, risk-taking, acts of service, reciprocity and communication make up the sub-themes of Relationship, which speaks to the intentional socioemotional linkages erotic beings forge with each other. Finally, Positive Affect covers the affirming emotions individuals feel about themselves and others they find relationship with.

Neither Exuded Being nor Sensory Experience can exist without originating in the mind or body of at least one animate Erotic Self. It is the Erotic Self that sits at the core of one's sexuality and is chiefly responsible for naming, defining, charting and assessing the course of one's sexiness development. Erotic Selves are neither attracted nor attractive automatically to all other individuals; in most cases, however, Erotic Selves use their attractions to achieve ideal sensory experiences. All human beings possess an Erotic Self, though its expression is moderated by any number of factors, including but not limited to age-appropriateness, self-esteem, level of erotic awareness and level of erotic intention. As many as six separate personalities for the Erotic Self emerged in this sample: Doers, Be-ers, Relators, Magnets, Products and Sexual Brands.

From the perspective of most respondents in this study, sexiness is ideally experienced in the exact way she/he/hir wishes in all desired settings and contexts. Achieving sexiness, however, does not occur without interference, much of which has the potential to directly influence an individual's sexiness development process or understanding thereof. Individuals may, for example, find their exudation amplified by connection with a loving kink community. They may also, in another instance, find their sense of sensual pleasure weakened by an unexpected personal or familial medical diagnosis. When an individual experiences a shift in sexiness frequency that is brought about by a force outside of themselves, they are said to be experiencing an External Influence.

I have attempted to thoroughly explain the dimensions and overall makeup of this model as well as provide several examples of how it functions in the lived experiences of people within the sample. In the final chapter of this book, I will provide an overview of what incorporation of Black Sexual Epistemology might signify, not just for the academy but also for Black scholars, sexuality scholars, sexuality practitioners and the public at large.

References

Brant, R. S. T., & Tisza, V. B. (1977). The sexually misused child. *American Journal of Orthopsychiatry, 47*(1), 80–90. https://doi.org/10.1111/j.1939-0025.1977.tb03247.x

Martinson, F. M. (1994). *The sexual life of children*. Westport, CT: Bergin & Garvey.

7

BSE IN CONTEXT

A Tool for Black Sexual Development

In the final chapter of his seminal text, Exploring Black Sexuality (2006),[1] legendary scholar Robert Staples presents a discussion on the state and future of sexuality among African Americans, including several predictions of how it will evolve over the coming years. Most of these forecasts are situational, focused on both behavioral expectations and evolutions in thought and attitude. Many of Staples's assertions are also debatable, even problematic in nature, including alarming claims about increases in children born out of wedlock, losses of marriageable Black men to homosexuality, shifts in Black female fellatio practices to compete for Black men with their white counterparts, rises in "pseudo-lesbianism" (183)[2] and the supposed legal entrapment of Black men through increases in sexual assault legislation. Engaging in debate is not the purpose of this book; however, as one of the few academic works focusing specifically on the issue of sexuality in Black communities, it is critical to point to the limitations of EBS's conjectures and position as a whole, particularly in the ways they mirror sociological analyses of old (Frazier, 1948; Moynihan, 1965), which relied on mischaracterizing and pathologizing Black people themselves in an effort to address legitimate yet unrelated challenges occurring within Black communities.

While it is not my intention to overstate the influence of the present volume, it is my hope that what is offered here serves just as adequately as Staples's work in laying out a future for Black sexuality that relates to its *sexological* evolution and not just sociopolitical factors. Indeed, while issues of family structure, sexual health status and access to wealth are all of significant concern to many African communities around the world, so, too, is the issue of sexual development itself—including identifying the priorities and needs of those who live and experience sexual desire and behavior on a daily basis. Moreover, in contrast to the starkly negative, myopic focus of my predecessor, what I present here is an attempt to articulate an understanding of Black sexual experiences that is balanced, inclusive and insistent on charting a hopeful trajectory. In the final chapter of this text, I discuss this research and how it fits within existing theoretical positions in human sexuality and Black studies, including those centered on its more applied and practical aspects. I revisit the ideas discussed throughout this book, expanding them to propose a working model for thinking about Black sexuality and African American-centered sexual development. I conclude by providing implications, limitations and opportunities for future research.

Contextualizing Blackness and Sexuality

As has been mentioned, this study is an offering to the canons of Black Studies and Sexology/Human Sexuality Studies. Race and sexuality have been fodder for productive discourse in both disciplines, yet significant gaps remain in the ways both conversations take place. Black Studies offers critical insight regarding the inextricable partnership between race and sexuality in both its interpersonal and sociopolitical navigation. Where the discipline falls short, however, is in theorizing most about the politics of sexual identity and public policy and least about the literality of copulating Black bodies. Indeed, while useful analyses of the social and visual representation of racialized sexuality and the racist biopolitics of empire abound within the literature, little to no scholarship that is explicitly theoretical about the concrete experience of sex proceeds from Black Studies, with even less devoted to the place of race within sexual epistemology.

To be fair, contemporary scholarship in Critical Black Studies (CBS) has made strides in casting light on this intellectual myopia (Battle & Barnes, 2005; Johnson & Henderson, 2005; McBride, 2005; Snorton, 2014; Wilson, 2016). The present work is offered as a challenge to both Black and human sexuality studies to engage with its collective oversight. With regard to sexual orientation and identity in particular, scholars raise critical questions about the ways that racism, sexism, homophobia and transphobia continue to erect axes of power against the marginalized even within the discipline. At the same time such critique remains equally limited in focus, centered more on teasing out the theoretical machinations of power and issues of identity than on theorizing about sexual activity and advancing alternatives to restrictive norms. The current aim of CBS is useful and even necessary for calling out this perpetuation of harm within the discipline; however, more remains to be seen in terms of new knowledge that can be practically applied outside of its intellectual borders.

By contrast, sexology has enjoyed an arguable monopoly on the explication of sexual phenomena. This proprietorship has grown solid enough to cover nearly all sexological imagination—not only what one does but also how one names that experience, negotiates or interprets its significance and identifies the actors involved and how, by extension, one should feel about one's experiences. As the first discipline to take up sexual inquiry in a systematic, intendedly unbiased way, it follows that this dominance is more arbitrary than deliberate. That said, this field relies on established "truths" about sexual epistemology that are often divorced from sociocultural nuance. As a whole, the discipline rarely, if ever, contends with the Eurocentric exclusivity on which its ontological standards have been created. In the process, it misses key opportunities to effectively interrogate what sex is and means to people who do not fit a Eurotypical norm.

Race, Power and Sexuality Practitionership

To reiterate, sexological scholarship has played an integral role in wielding knowledge toward the establishment of authoritative social sexual norms in many, if not most, parts of the Western world. Scholars and practitioners alike recognize the discipline as one from which much of the contemporary world's understanding of sexuality and sexual normalcy takes its cues (Bullough, 1994). Though subject to criticism from nonacademic detractors, most U.S. sociosexual advances of the last 60-plus years emerged from the influential work of sexological scientist–practitioners, including Alfred Kinsey, William Masters and Virginia Johnson, Beverly Whipple and Milton Diamond (Bullough, 1994; Weeks, 1985). Sexology has asserted itself over time as a contemporary discourse leader even while resting on ideologically based, socially constructed notions of biological reality and its significance (Weeks, 1985).

Sexology's birth as a field could be said to have also been one of an intellectual culture given the ways that its scholars have used their science over time to advocate for new and distinct social norms within other areas of social life—for example, the legal system, public policy and pop culture (Bullough, 1994). From this position, sexologists have gained license to categorize and codify sexual behavior alongside previous standing institutions, yielding their own forms of power–knowledge. In fact, I contend that sexology's reliance on the elevated status of empirical research established it early on as worthy of holding unprecedented legitimacy for making assertions about the nature of sexual reality (Bullough, 1994). Though perhaps not consciously unified in this effort, the work of early sexological professionals was, in fact, an effort that indirectly implied, in the words of anthropologist Bronislaw Malinowski, "a correct idea of what sexual life means to a people" (Weeks, 1985, 100).[3] This ability to lead social narratives about normative sexuality carries major implications, both for those centered in and those disallowed from the discourse, including, again, African Americans. One area in which this privilege carries significant weight in and repercussions for the present day is sex and sexuality education.

From its beginnings in the late 1800s, sexuality education in the United States has served as its own appointed authority for the establishment and dissemination of legitimate sexual knowledge (Carrera, 1971). In its earliest days, sex education fit within "the general field of morals"[4] and was in most—if not all—cases linked predominantly to the prevention of venereal diseases. Over time, this perspective evolved to include a much wider range of topics and goals, including marriage and family preparation, pregnancy prevention and, more recently—in rare cases—embodying more positive sexual attitudes (Breuss & Greenberg, 2009). At the same time, a review of many present-day platforms utilized in the classroom among sex educators reveals a fundamental impetus to influence how individuals think about and respond to sexuality, which carries significant implications for the country's collective cultural discourse around sexuality and sexual epistemology (Woo et al., 2011).

It is worth reviewing the relationship between sexuality practitionership and public health, as most, if not all, of the most well-known and well-respected sex education initiatives are informed by public health theory and research (Carrera, 1971; Rosen, 1958). This is not to say that all sex education is informed by public health; that it is not is significant to the degree that it helps distinguish between various schools of thought relative to conceptualizing sexual health. For instance, prevention is an inherent aspect of public health, as the field itself was first conceived with the notion to address both current and future threats of disease in the common populace (Duffy, 1990; Rosen, 1958). To the average public health professional, true health is gauged by the absence of disease and other predetermined factors deemed to threaten one's life span (Evans, 2010). Preventive education exists, however, in contrast to other education models, including those focused on sexual wellness and sexual relationship enhancement. Within sex therapy, for example, sexual satisfaction is the primary aim, with more attention paid to enhancing the quality of one's life and not necessarily the quantity thereof. Linwood Lewis (2004) discusses this as the dichotomy of preventive versus eudaemonic sexual health discourse, citing public health as responsible for a disproportionate application of the former in non-white populations.

The particular advancement of sex education within African American communities cannot be fully understood without proper attention to the social hygiene movement of the late 1800s and early 1900s. Groups like the American Social Hygiene Association are credited with creating the first sex education programs in Black communities; it is significant that they were largely advanced with the goal of alleviating the spread of venereal diseases. It was believed by most leaders of the time that the spread of diseases like syphilis and gonorrhea represented a moral prevalence over any other kind. Moreover, efforts to temper their spread in African Americans were fueled as much by concerns about the perceived "effects" of inherent Black hypersexuality rubbing off on White counterparts as by concern for the well-being of African Americans. Sharma (2010)[5] notes that there were some within ASHA who, over time, would come to not hold such extreme racist ideals, attributing differences in prevalence rates to systemic inequities like poverty and limited or compromised medical access. As noted elsewhere, however, even these more sympathetic views of disease in the Black community rested on the assumed lower status of Black people—an as yet unchecked perspective that I argue has lent itself to the perpetuation of prevention as a foundational goal of most, if not all, sexuality practitioner initiatives advanced in Black communities over time.

The dominance of public health over sexuality practitionership in African American communities, Lewis argues, has created an overemphasis on STI and pregnancy prevention (as some examples) as primary means for maintaining sexual health, to the detriment of pedagogical coverage of eudaemonic topics, including pleasure, emotional balance and relationship satisfaction (Lewis, 2004). "By focusing on these problems," he continues, "researchers strengthen the association between danger to the public body and the sexual behavior of persons of ethnic minority background" (226).[6] Lewis is clear that when sexology practitioners do not engage African Americans through a eudaemonic lens, the field as a whole is left with lopsided impressions about what constitutes normative and ideal sexual experience among the population. Moreover, the intellectual privilege sexuality practitioners exert through a power–knowledge framework makes it so that these impressions become easily reified in all future interactions with the population. Rightfully noting that the majority of African American people do not experience extreme adverse consequences as a result of sexual engagement, Lewis ultimately exposes the inherent anti-Blackness in preventive sexual health discourse and offers a solution to the issue by refocusing the lens of sexual health research to include a larger diversity of African American voices.

Theory Summary

Black Sexual Epistemology represents the themes and mechanisms present in the navigation of sexuality among African American people. It is a theory that specifically centers African American people and is meant to articulate Black cultural experiences. Sexuality among African Americans represents the sum total of relationships, expressions and experiences navigated in the fulfillment of sexiness. Sexiness may be pursued or it may occur unintentionally; an assessment of sexiness requires only one other individual to perceive and assess it as such. Sexiness can emerge as one of eight channels, fitting within the areas of Exuded Being or Sensory Experience. Individuals may intend to reach one or two channels of sexiness or actively work to pursue all eight; optimal volume for any one channel is a form of sexiness to any individual who encounters and perceives it as such. Each individual sits as the primary actor at the center of their sexual universe. This individual, the Erotic Self, is capable of making assessments of sexiness in one's self and environment while picking and choosing the encounters that gain them perceived closest access to the channels of sexiness that matter to them.

Race is a significant part of the sexual universe of African Americans in both affirmative and deleterious ways. On one level, Performative Blackness is an aspect of sexiness witnessed in Black bodies and culturally specific ways of being. From melanin-rich skin and full lips to assertions of cool and confidence, many African Americans perceive specialness in Black people, separating them qualitatively from other groups. By contrast, racialization is a persistent moderating factor in African Americans' attainment of sexiness, such that many find themselves challenged by racism in their ability to fully access it. Tropes about Black sexual bodies put many African Americans in a hypersensitive space in which they may police their own or others' sexuality or have their own sexual universe policed. Resistance of racialization's adverse effects is not only part of the African American sexual universe but also a tool often employed in sexiness development. Racialization is not the only external influence on African American sexual experience; however, it is a common, if not the most common, influence. Other external influences on individual sexiness development, which can be positive, negative and neutral, include personal illness, relationship status, technological access, sexual trauma and misuse, sexual precocity and commercialism. There is no present limit, however, to all the ways that sexiness fulfillment can be moderated within an individual's life.

The Erotic Self is the agentic being at the center of one's sexuality and is named according to that self's relationship to sexiness and the sexual universe. For most, the relationship is subjective, driven chiefly by the individual's self-perception. In other cases, the relationship is objective, determined by how that self is perceived by others. At least six different personas were identified in this study: Doer/Be-er, Journeyer, Relator, Product, Object and Sexual Brand. These do not, however, represent the complete list of personas accessible to the population. The persona assigned to or taken on by an erotic self may determine what one expects from one's self and other players in one's sexual universe.

Proposing a Working Model of Black Sexuality/African American-Centered Sexual Development

Black Sexual Epistemology (BSE) is an analysis that can speak to a wide range of disciplines yet is most situated at the intersection of human sexuality studies and Black studies. To be clear, it is a critical framework that provides a new way of looking at both the sexuality of African American people and, potentially, sexuality as a whole. I have already offered critiques of both fields to clarify specific gaps to which the present work could be applied. What I propose now is an explanation of what new knowledge the present research provides along with how it directly challenges standing intellectual norms. To begin, BSE is a theory of embodiment, extending from a foundational consideration of, to use Cunningham's (2010) phrasing, "material sex."[7] It is, at present, the first and only known theoretical model of its kind. It specifically theorizes about the body's engagement with "sexiness," or the "stuff" of sex—i.e., the product of the body's encountering of other bodies/erotic beings. While sexuality is constitutive of a full conceptual universe (thoughts, intentions, labels, relationships and other sensory representations), I argue that it is most simply condensable to the actions of bodies—how they show up in the world and with whom and how they interact with other physical entities. In talking about sexuality within this particular research study, it was important to me that the analysis begin here, as it is the concept that, in my estimation, is most taken for granted within both academic and popular sexuality discourses.

When most people talk about the sexual activities of human bodies, it is assumed that they are referring to coitus, which is loosely defined as "sexual intercourse" and most commonly refers to the interactions of one's genitals (Breuss & Greenberg, 2009). In fact, one could argue, even without stating so explicitly, that the whole field of sexuality practitionership has centered on this experience, indirectly prioritizing it as the sole assumed means through which individuals achieve sexual fulfillment. An application of BSE challenges us to reposition the capacity and norm of sexual fulfillment in a myriad of arenas outside of the genitals, expanding what is presently assumed about coitus's "nature." For example, when stripped down to the more essentialized notions of "exuded being" and "sensory experience," one might be able to see "coitus" in numerous atypical activities—for example, a pickup basketball game between friends or a fan enjoying a concert by their favorite music performer. In both experiences, the individual encounters the exudation volume of the entity/entities with whom they come in contact and achieves some type of sensory experience (sensual pleasure is one obvious example but perhaps some of the other channels as well).

A willingness to conceptually deconstruct and reconstruct our understanding of sex in this way has the potential to expand our understanding of what it means to be "sexually healthy" as well as increase our understanding of sex's function and significance in an individual's life. If sexiness can emerge through all things (including the nonpornographic), then it essentially cannot and should not be hidden, but rather normalized, even celebrated. From this broadened perspective, sexiness takes its place as a chief vehicle for not only reproduction but also for all manner of whole-life fulfillment.

BSE is a model that accounts for the role and salience of race in the lives of African American people. It recognizes that race, and specifically the experience of racialization, does play a significant part in one's sexual navigation. The experience of living in the world as a racialized person, with all of the socialization into anti-Blackness and White supremacy, directly impacts how one is taught to view one's sexual self, what one is drawn to sexually and what one contends with in the desire to pursue sexual encounters. This influence can be adverse, causing limitations in one's ability to access the full field of eligible dating or sexual partners one desires or motivating one to question one's attractiveness in comparison to others who more readily fit the norms of conventional beauty. This influence can also be affirmative, sparking a certain pride in the individual's cultural uniqueness, or an active resistance against deleterious external messaging. BSE does not assume the quantitative influence of race on the individual more than it allows space for an authentic dialogical unpacking and reconciliation of race's role within an individual's sexual development experience. This is a departure from present models of sexuality that do not account for race at all.

BSE is also a model for articulating a eudemonic, life-affirming Black sexuality, proceeding with the intention to develop, not prevent, the sexual expression of the population. Within this model, exhibiting sexiness is a matter of wellness given its conceptual connection to enjoyed or attractive things and the generally positive assessment it receives. Facilitated as a dialogical process, BSE invites African Americans to explore important questions they've currently lacked the privilege to explore: "what is sexiness to me?" "In what ways do I or can I access sexiness in my life?" "What do I *want* sexiness to look like in my life?" "What stops or has stopped me from cultivating sexiness, and can those barriers be addressed?" "Could cultivating particular channels of sexiness improve my quality of life, and if so, how?" and, finally, "What would it mean to become intentional about developing personal sexiness?" As can be seen by the diversity of the sample, these are questions that can be answered regardless of an individual's sexual orientation or experience. And while it does not assume that sexual problems don't exist or matter, it repositions these challenges in a way that avoids overinflating their ability to deter the sexiness development process. In fact, this theory encourages personal agency in the evolution of the erotic self *despite* challenges. Moreover, it recognizes that many of the challenges experienced by the erotic self may, in fact, be alleviated through the active development of sexiness or the growth and maturity of one's exuded being and sensory experience.

Finally, it must be clarified that while BSE is a model that could be effectively considered by any individual, it is expressly meant for the target population, which is to say that it is first and foremost a theory about Black people. It comes from the voices of a wide range of Black individuals of varying sexual orientations, gender identities, body sizes and socioeconomic statuses. Because this research used race as the sole moderating variable of inquiry, it is important to stress that this theory is intersectional and directly inspired by E. Patrick Johnson's (2005) "quare" theory.[8] The inclusion of heterosexually identified people within the study sample precludes BSE from being legitimately called quare in total; however, it does assert itself as a model for individuals fitting within the part of Johnson's definition that includes "one for whom sexual and gender identities always already intersect with racial subjectivity" (125).[9]

I am aware that asserting a Black queer-informed model that is meant for all Black people puts it at risk of co-opting or being co-opted as a means to privilege the racialized experiences of Black, cisgender, heterosexual individuals over other African Americans. What is clear from the data, however, and from most other critical Black studies perspectives, is that systems of oppression are inextricably intertwined, meaning that efforts to unpack the effects of racism on an individual's sexiness trajectory cannot be detached from those that simultaneously implicate sexism, heterosexism/homophobia, classism, cissexism/transphobia, colorism, fatphobia, ableism and the like. An application of this theory in which only part of the African American population—*any* part—is considered to speak for the whole deviates from the foundation on which it stands. However, while privileged individuals within African American communities are invited to use the model to make declarations about their own experiences, they should also be challenged to ask how they might use BSE elements to perpetuate harm against or marginalize others in their sexiness development, whether through direct or indirect means.

Intellectual/Research Implications

In a general sense, Black Sexual Epistemology is one theoretical model that increases our present understanding of sexuality as a life span experience. Specifically, it provides concrete evidence to support the notion that race emerges with sexuality as an intersecting experience for the average African American individual. This is a departure not only from sexuality models that neglect to consider race but also from theories that center on one particular "at-risk" subset of the population, focus on its immaterial aspects or are meant to examine some type of sexual infirmity. In successfully establishing race as a salient factor in the normative lived experience of sex for at least one population in the world, a foundation is set to perhaps more adequately consider how race factors into the human sexual experience at large as well as other aspects of sexuality and sexual health not as a spurious "biological determinant" but as the social influence it has been shown to be.

Scope of Relevance

The present research provides a scope of relevance that expands the sexuality discourse in some areas, while fine-tuning it in others. On one level, it broadens the scope of relevance to cover normative lived experience versus pathology or sexual problems. As has been noted here and by previous sexology scholars, the broader study of sexuality from a dysfunction and disorder focus has created an intellectual void in the canon in which little to nothing is known about how everyday people go about considering, or even conducting, their sexual lives (Booth, 2014). That said, the present research also *expands* the idea of "sexual problem" in a thought-provoking way, including new areas that have had limited consideration in the past. This second expansion relates to my latter point that this present research adds a dimension ("race") to the discourse that simultaneously helps the larger concept ("sexuality") be more easily delineated in its application. From this research, it is better understood that while sexual activities, for example, may be commonly practiced, the phenomenology of sex and how it is conceptualized are not universal and cut across social lines in significant ways. To reiterate, this research as well as BSE, its resulting theory, does not postulate about all human beings; however, it does present new possibilities for imagining the human sexual experience, which could subsequently be considered with other populations.

Black Studies

BSE is, quite clearly, a theory fitting within the tradition of Black Studies. It is directly articulated for and by Black people for the chief purpose of bettering their lived experiences. Several theories of Black sexuality have been included in this book. The present model, however, represents the first that a) theorizes specifically about the epistemological experience of sexiness and b) attempts to establish operational ideas that may prove resonant for the entire population. These points are significant for the ways they address the ontological demands of Blackness, which at present are still, at best, in their infancy. The historical intellectual treatment of African American people is such that they are "nonexistent" ontologically. While they do have a presence within the imagination of whiteness, this existence is unreliable at best and illegitimate at worst, as it is merely an idea and not indicative of a material lived experience (Sithole, 2016).

BSE provides a basis for continued explorations of Black ontology by offering ideas that are material in nature and can thus be expanded through future discourse and study. Moreover, and perhaps in spite of the perpetuity of the White gaze, BSE is a Black *sexological* theory through which African American people may look through their own eyes at their sexuality—their exuded being, their sensory experiences and their sexual universe—as they imagine it to be, in real time. By some estimations, Blackness as a subjective status is an irreversible condition to which the humanity of African people cannot be effectively reconciled (Sithole, 2016). BSE sits in relation to this perspective, however, as both a theoretical and methodological model for what could be a way forward in forging an empowered Black sexual future that actively resists the mainstream.

Because BSE is a sexological theory that is meant for all Black people, it also backs up the progression of a Black sexual studies research agenda that limits the emphasis to women and queer subjects. While that body of scholarship is useful and necessary, I argue that it cannot preclude the equally necessary work of understanding how racism and racialization have positioned all Black people as a sexual "other" with regard to mainstream populations. Indeed, as E. Patrick Johnson (2003) asserts, "When black Americans have employed the rhetoric of black authenticity, the outcome has often been a political agenda that has excluded more voices than it has included" (3).[10] Further research that explores sex and race and their relationship to all Black people may help us to better identify varying gradations of their effects on all subpopulations and to even highlight pathways between sexualized racism and other intracultural marginalizations.

Human Sexuality

The foundational elements of BSE normalize sex and sexuality in a way that shifts how we might be able to discuss them in the future, particularly in relationship to sex positivity and its opposite, sex negativity. At present, there is no standard definition of either concept, with current perspectives varying in focus between knowledge, skill and attitude (Ivanski & Kohut, 2017). BSE, however, is an inherently sex positive model because it recognizes sexiness as a valid, aspirational aspect of an individual's personal development and wellness. Sexiness and, by extension, sexuality are seen through this model as inextricable qualities of every aspect of life, not just copulation. The themes of sexiness in BSE assert the primacy of one's optimal exuded being and sensory experience, the particularities of both being self-determinative. Through this notion, one should be able to see a conceptualization of sex positivity in which "autonomy, acceptance and consent" are inherent (items identified as common parts of most sex positivity definitions) but also to which joy, personal development and self-mastery are added. Indeed, the themes presented through the model represent aspects in life that feel good to people, that they enjoy, to which they are attracted and of which they want to experience greater amounts, both quantitatively and qualitatively.

When pursuit of BSE's themes occurs in a way that is self-defined and then achieved, the accomplishment is one that adds quality to the individual's life, thus making it a "positive." Moreover, with a broadening of sexiness to encompass non-copulative activities, the potential for both reaching it and removing the stigma of reaching it is increased, as sexiness development becomes a more normalized, validated intention. With all of this in mind, the goals of a sex positive society become clearer, in that greater acceptance of the goodness and universality of sexuality emerges hand in hand with the promoted development of individually derived, autonomous expressions of exuded self and sensory experience. By extension, the converse, sex negativity, also shifts, becoming more explicative of a denial of sexuality's ubiquity and an erection of those elements (interpersonal, structural and otherwise) that work to block one's sexiness development trajectory. This imperative, coincidentally, is not only directly connected to the reported lived experience and intentions of individuals within this sample but is also supportive of the original intentions of comprehensive sex education, which focus on the development of positive, life-affirming sexuality (Goldfarb, 2009).

Social Discourses

Because of the way it directly consults and prioritizes the sexological musings of Afro-descended people, there is a potential for BSE to trigger a shift in current popular discourses on sex. As it stands, African American people are still, by and large, excluded as architects in popular American discourses about sex. This is not to say that they are not referenced, however, as Black culture continues to influence pop culture even while Black people themselves are not allowed to lead its trajectory (Cooper, 2018; Stephens & Phillips, 2003). Anti-Blackness theorists have clarified how the white imago of Blackness supersedes Black self-conceptualization by silencing its truth with distorted interpretations of the Black body (Sithole, 2016; Yancy, 2008). Employment of BSE as a dialogical tool could potentially facilitate a more thoughtful absorption of Black sexual expression among non-Black others. This is, albeit, a lofty assertion at best; however, what the present research confirms is that African American people have a vested interest in articulating ideals about sex and sexuality and should thus be given ample opportunity to have those ideas heard and validated.

Practitioner Implications

The possibility of an alternative sexuality model that prioritizes sexiness development has major implications for those who serve African American populations. As was already mentioned, the preventive model that permeates most sex practitioner discourses disproportionately affects African Americans (Lewis, 2004). Moreover, contemporary models of sexuality intervention, whether they be comprehensive or otherwise, still establish sexual abstinence as the ideal, regardless of context (Connell & Elliott, 2009; Goldfarb, 2009). A consideration of BSE might help restructure a basis for sexuality practitionership that more accurately reflects contemporary lived experiences. For example, within sex education it is possible to affirm exuded being and sensory experience without being prescriptive. If teachers were allowed to take on a more wholesale intention based on validating one's expressed ownership and expression of these elements, this may allow them space to shift away from prescriptive intentions that tell students *what* to think and toward intentions that help students learn *how* to think about sexuality, which also supports a more empowered sexiness development trajectory. Goldfarb (2009)[11] reminds us of the present challenge faced by sexuality educators in forging a common identity that effectively stands against the unambiguous political perspective of sexual conservatives. A consideration of BSE in practice may effectively facilitate the capacity to develop that message.

Sex Education

It is important to reiterate that this research extends directly from the reports of individuals' lived experiences and conceptual priorities. As such, if it is known that present models of sex education in African American communities focus predominantly on pregnancy or STI prevention, then from the present research we should be able to safely say that current pedagogical models are inadequate in addressing the topics and concerns on the minds of most African American people. Understanding this, then, is not only a moral concern but also a practical one: why would we want to continue to invest resources into the prioritization of pedagogical concepts that are not resonant and are, as such, less likely to be integrated? Indeed, cultural competence in sex education should not only address the language and colloquial style of the community in question but also successfully speak to its present and anticipated priorities.

In speaking about the future of sexuality education, Elizabeth Schroeder (2009)[12] identifies seven major lessons that the field would do well to consider. While all seven are of considerable importance, two relate specifically to the present research, ideas for each I will expound on here. To begin, Schroeder asserts that sexuality education needs a "makeover" that more effectively articulates its intentions and accomplishments as well as expectations for those who practice it. I have already suggested a way forward with regard to the field's pedagogical intentions. Additionally, the present model provides justification for asserting the expectation that sexuality educators develop an awareness of how White supremacy, anti-Blackness, racialized sexuality and sexualized racism play out in the work they do. Within this makeover, Schroeder also asserts that sexuality education be effectively integrated into all subjects and that adults and caregivers be included in the teaching process. The establishment of sexuality's ubiquity within this model provides an additional support for this suggestion. To the latter point, I would assert that adults and caregivers not only be included in teaching but also be considered as co-developers in the learning process given lapses that may exist in their own sexiness development to date.

Much of my response to the first of Schroeder's points overlaps with the second, which I am interested in here—that sexuality education need be more diverse in content and pedagogical approach. I am in wholehearted agreement with her declaration that "[i]t is imperative that sexuality educators learn to always be thinking of 'the other,' whomever that 'other' may be, and to use language and examples that include more than the power majority—heterosexual, white, able-bodied, and so on" (262).[13] Black people, and African Americans in particular, are far too often the unspoken "other" in sex education spaces, whether in a comprehensive or abstinence-only classroom and whether they are alone or with other non-Black learners. As Connell and Elliott (2009)[14] note, Black children are those who are most often conceptualized as "corrupting" and "hypersexual"—the bad others whose behavior is meant to be avoided by "innocent" and good children. In all-Black spaces, these children become even more stratified by gender, class, sexual orientation and, in some cases, nation of origin. A classroom informed by BSE has the potential to shift the stigma Black children receive in the sex ed classroom by shifting the common discourse toward one in which all children are challenged to grow in their critical thinking about sexiness, sexuality and race and, by extension, Black children are allowed the normalization and validation of experience they have yet to fully receive. Ultimately, the present research supports a perspective Schroeder (2009) outlines succinctly: "the topic of sexuality must be addressed from a developmental and normative standpoint, rather than focusing exclusively on sexual dysfunctions, assault survival, and so-called 'deviancy' as too many programs do" (259). BSE provides a speculative conceptual model on which practical, culturally responsive and socially just pedagogical goals could be built.

Sexuality Counseling and Therapy

Outside the classroom, BSE carries several implications and uses for clinical professionals. As individuals charged with the task of facilitating growth and healing on the micro-level, BSE provides a general model therapists can use to help both clients and couples imagine ideal sexual experiences and craft goals to accomplish over time. Beyond theoretical consideration, BSE gives clinicians a working personal assessment tool that can be used both inside and outside the therapeutic space, being routinely consulted for adjustments as necessary. And in using ideas that come directly from the imagination of average individuals, BSE also gives clients practical language to name personal experiences they might not have been able to conceptualize in other ways. Finally, although BSE centers lived experience among African Americans, individuals in relationship with African Americans may find its concepts useful for better understanding the contextual dimensions of their lives with these individuals.

Black Sexual Epistemology lends credence to the use of Hardy and Laszloffy's (2002)[15] multicultural perspective (MCP) in therapeutic practice. In particular, it highlights the salience of race as having contextual, ambivalent influence on the individual, whether unpacking fetishization in an interracial marriage, as one example, or constructing sexual self-esteem based on one's desired embodiment of perceived cultural identity. As MCP's creators note, "There is a virtually inextricable relationship between context and reality, in that context shapes our reality, and it defines and punctuates the meanings we attach to our lives" (51).[16] BSE gives explicit permission for race to be named and discussed as part of the client's context and thus their lived reality. At the same time, Blackness is positioned within the BSE model as a phenomenon that is universal only in theoretical possibility, allowing space for the client to more accurately define its application to their own personal life. BSE makes no assumptions about how racialization matters to the client, except to acknowledge and validate its potentiality within the individual's social context.

Which brings me to the final point. Probing deeper, BSE is a framework that pushes the envelope for the clinical sexuality practitioner, challenging them to become more responsive to clients' racially informed therapeutic needs. This note is particularly significant in light of the MCP tenet asserting the importance of cross-cultural negotiation in the therapist–client relationship.[17] Present research supports the theory that white clinicians are not comfortable addressing racism and racialized experiences with their clients of color (Tuckwell, 2002; Moodley, Lago, & Talahite, 2004).[18,19] Moreover, there is a growing sentiment that white clinicians are not willing to address their own discomforts around race in professional settings, growing more silent about it in instances when they are buttressed by lack of racial diversity or recognition at the organizational level (Jackson, 2018).[20] Models like BSE that inherently center racialized people may do well to facilitate both learning and empathy where they otherwise fail to emerge. While some scholars have called this into question, even going so far as to suggest that mentioning race borders on racist behavior itself, others assert avoidance to be the true racism and suggest that to avoid explicit inclusion of race is not only incompetent practice but also an unethical disservice to the client (McKenzie-Mavinga, 2018).[21]

Social Work and Other Helping Professions

The overwhelming number and diversity of careers included under the title "helping professions" limit my ability to speculate about the relevance of this model for this type of work in any comprehensive way. I would be remiss, however, not to invite this group to consider how BSE might assist in elucidating how sexuality and race emerge in the social contexts of the clients they serve. In his 1983 offering *The Sexual Dimension: A Guide for the Mental Health Practitioner*, Herbert Strean (1983)[22] offered two important ideas related to the salience of sexuality in the average person's life. Specifically, he suggested that a) the quality of an individual's sexual functioning is a by-product of their attitude about themselves and their relationships with others and that b) many (if not most) of the general concerns raised by clients served by helping professionals are, at their core, rooted in underlying psychosexual challenges. Accepting the interrelationship between race and sex provides a new avenue of possibility for the helping professional in attempting to better understand the psychosexual source of their clients' concerns and needs. Particularly for those who may present with "problems" in this area, BSE may do well to facilitate increased understanding of sexual phenomena experienced within African American communities and allow helping professionals to invite race, racialization and even sexiness into the conversation as an influence warranting further reflection and confrontation.

Assumptions and Limitations

From the beginning, this study emerged from the assumption that one overarching theory of sexuality could be developed that successfully articulates the experiences of all African American people—an admittedly large, ambitious assertion. That this assertion is so large and ambitious explains the many arms of BSE's subsequent structure. An additional assumption made through this study was that a model of sexuality could be successfully conceived through the etymological frame of "sexiness." While this assumption proved salient for many within the study, it was ultimately determined that sexiness could not fully capture the bigger picture. Sexuality is ultimately described in this work as a "universe" precisely because it cannot be easily contained by one concrete activity or experience; sexiness, by extension, has a relationship to sexuality that still represents an accurate articulation of the data. That said, regardless of how it was able to be contained and articulated through the present model, there may still be individuals for whom sexiness and its described attributes—exuded being and sensory experience—have no true conceptual reference point. Continued research on the topic will determine a point at which the model's parts may need to be adjusted.

Sex Positivity

As mentioned, it was assumed from the very beginning of this study that sex and sexuality had meaning for the population that was both salient and positive. This centering was largely guided by my background as a sexologist trained in the promotion of sexual wellness as well as my own culturally informed experience of Black sexuality. While it appears that said assumptions resonated with those who participated, it is important to stress that these data may be potentially skewed by a sample of individuals who have an overinflated enthusiasm for sex and sexuality that is different from others within the population. In terms of alleviating this in the future, it may be inherently difficult to engage individuals who do not have a sex-positive lens, who would be more likely to refrain from participating in sexuality research altogether. Further research, however, might do well to elucidate potential differences between those who explicitly identify as sex-positive or sex affirming and those who have more conservative or sex-negative views.

Salience of Blackness and Race Oversight

Another inherent assumption within the initial conceptualization of this study regarded the degree to which race and Blackness specifically were assumed to matter to the lives of African American people. Indeed, in my focus on remaining unbiased in the interpretation of information, I neglected to see the inherent bias of my research agenda itself, projecting my own quantitative experience of race onto the conversations I anticipated having with others. I was fortunate, in that Blackness emerged as a consistently salient element of identity for respondents in the sample; however, much of that coincidence can be likely linked to the explicit title of the study, which could have deterred African Americans who are not as interested in race or who do not see it as an integral aspect of their identity. It is important to acknowledge that Blackness may not be a resonant cultural marker for all people of African American descent. To clarify any differences that remain, future studies may wish to compare conceptions of sexiness between those for whom Blackness is salient and those for whom it is not.

At the same time I assert this point, I'd like to return to the story of Mary, the engaged respondent I discussed in Chapter Two. At the beginning of our conversation, Mary was adamant that while race was a significant influencing factor in society at large, it was not as influential in her sexual universe, asserting that "[w]hen I think of my sexuality or sexiness in general, I don't put a color toward it. . . . As far as my own personal experience, I can't really correlate the two." When given the chance later in our conversation to share more from her lived experience, however, the story she shared would come to reveal more about the true nature of race's implicit influence on her sexual life:

> [s]o my fiancé, like, he's dated all types of women, right? He's dated Black women, of course, White women. He grew up in an all-white neighborhood—Asian, Latino and so on. Sometimes, I think like, oh my god, like sometimes I'm like, "Oh my God, I *really* don't feel like doing it today. I *really* don't." Right? And then I think, "He's been with white girls. Girl—you gotta put that head down, you gotta give him head like *insane, crazy* because he's—[*laughs*]—and we've been together for, like, four years, but I still think like, "Oh my God—OH MY GOD, I gotta, like, REALLY, um, do it WELL, like, because he's probably used to that.

Mary went on to explain how this internal back and forth dialogue she's experienced is an occasional source of anxiety for her relative to her concern about her partner's overall sexual satisfaction in the relationship. In reviewing her full interview it became clear that while race did have real-time influence on Mary's sexual experience and decision-making, its effect was not readily apparent to her even after significant probing on my part as the researcher. In this way, it is important to understand that, in some cases, race may still be a salient operating factor in the sexual universe of someone who asserts it isn't if for no other reason that, like a fish in water, they are too submerged within the parameters of their racialized world to fully see it.

Intentionally Non-Diasporic

Extending from my last point about the assumed salience of Blackness, this study is limited by design to focus explicitly on people who identify as African American. To be clear, this was done both to simplify the data analysis process and to acknowledge that while anti-Blackness is a global phenomenon, there are likely significant differences in how it emerges in the lives of African people across the diaspora, particularly those who did not descend from survivors of the Transatlantic Slave Trade. That said, my own awareness of this global salience combined with the particular instance of pushback I received from African people outside of the U.S. who were made aware of the study but felt they did not meet the established criteria, suggests that such a study might be easily replicable with Black people in other geographic locations. Coincidentally, a handful of respondents in this study did reveal during their interviews with me that they had ancestry from elsewhere in the African diaspora or were born in other parts of the diaspora before immigrating to the United States in childhood. While their backgrounds did not technically fit those of the individuals I anticipated speaking with, I made space for those who did sign up out of my own perception of potential diasporic overlap, my aforementioned understanding of global anti-Blackness and my respect for their self-identification with "African American" as an identity marker.

Demographics

This study benefitted from a richly diverse sample of participants, exhibiting a wide range of ages, localities of origin, localities of residence, genders and sexual orientations. That said, there are at least four areas of demographic information that were not captured, which presents an additional limitation in the interpretation of results. For one, no religious demographic data were collected from this sample—a grave oversight given the number of respondents who cited religion as a major influence on their ideas about race and sexuality. While I was able to capture intriguing data about religion's influence on those who volunteered it, questions remain about how respondents were affected by it at an earlier age, as well as how their religious identity has evolved over time. Responses to both questions could prove highly useful in future studies.

Second, there were a sizeable number of respondents (15) who reported having acquired a high school diploma; however, the failure to parse current educational experience (e.g., currently in college versus non-attending) misses some nuances that emerged within participant responses, including in the case of one respondent who had his high school diploma but was functionally illiterate. Future iterations of this study would do well to tease out those pieces of the data and to include questions related to socioeconomic status or family SES. Indeed, while the sample anecdotally reflects class diversity, it is not clear from the datasheets how the sample is distributed. In addition, given some theoretical perspectives on the intersecting relationships between class and sexual attitudes, there is some potential for class influence on respondent answers that has likely been missed in the present analysis. Finally, limitations in the resources available for data collection preempted plans to collect data from participants in the western and southwestern parts of the United States. Though such oversight might appear slight on the surface, subtle regional differences in response between those in New York and those in Wisconsin suggest that at least some regional limitations might be present in the interpretation of these data as well.

Emic Positionality/Epistemological Relationship

My final point is neither an assumption nor a limitation in the formal sense, though it is an important point nonetheless. I would be remiss in not mentioning the inherent benefit I was afforded as an African American in completing this particular research study. I conducted this research from an emic perspective, attempting to understand the perspective of individuals who share my ethnic background yet still experience it through their own particular lens (Morris et al., 1999).[23] Moreover, while I perceived a certain facility in being able to collect data as a racial "insider" before research commenced, I was taken aback by the extent of the epistemic relationship I would develop with participants during this study and with the data as a whole.

I began by intentionally establishing a safe, conversational space in which participants were made to feel they could openly and honestly share; that I was African American, I believe, made that space appear even more accessible and able to be trusted. In only one case did a participant express uncertainty about meeting with me; in this case, the individual ultimately canceled the interview altogether. With regard to everyone else, once we began to chat and they sat with my questions, enthusiasm for many expanded from being in the study and having their voices heard to unearthing discoveries that were new even to them, allowing us to make meaning *together* out of their words and stories. In many ways, my research participants and I were co-creators in this process, engaging in a persistent dialogical give and take that was as personally enlightening for them as it was for me. Most, if not all, members of the sample left their interview with an explicit desire to read the final study results. Much of this enthusiasm, I believe, came from the evolving vested interest they developed during our conversation to advance a new, arguably unprecedented conversation.

In their study of health attitudes among African American communities in North Carolina, Rajack-Talley et al. (2017)[24] address present debates about the use of race-based epistemologies in research—a practice that was inherent to the present work. Critics of race-based epistemologies argue that their employment encourages an ethnocentric bias in the data and their interpretation. However, I would argue that such positionality actually served an opposite function here, in that participants were less interested in speaking "for the race" and more interested in telling their own individual stories as they authentically experienced them. This latter point is consistent with the authors' assertion that the "distinct historical and cultural experiences of the African people" (414)[25] have limited African Americans' ability to be authentically depicted within the literature. The use of an emic research position ultimately served to alleviate the perpetuation of this history.

Opportunities for Future Research

Sexiness and Sexual Health

It is clear that sexiness is a resonant concept for members of this sample, one that may extend to other populations. This carries significant possibilities for improving the ways that sexual health is promoted within African American communities, particularly in relation to sexual wellness, sexual negotiation and STI prevention. For example, contraceptive use is a major tenet of STI prevention. If it were possible to shift prevention messaging to focus on the possibilities of sensual pleasure experienced through, say, proper condom application, such pivoting might go a long way toward increasing the likelihood that contraceptives are used as an enhancement to the sexiness experience.

On another note, what is also clear from the data is that, for many African Americans, Blackness is a sexy experience. Given its larger influence on popular culture, a curious question remains regarding the ways that Performative Blackness influences the conceptualization of non-Black groups both as subjects and, potentially, appropriating actors.

External Influences

There is no question that external influences, including anti-Black racism and White supremacy, serve as significant adverse influences on the sexiness experience of African American people. What is not entirely certain, however, is the full range of affects triggered by racialization as well as the psychological processes involved in the integration of these influences into the psyche. A classification system of race as an external influence might be useful for the purposes of helping newer generations of African American people better identify and articulate the experiences that happen to them so that they can perhaps be more easily reconciled. To the latter point, certain specific questions come to mind: is there a specific pathway, for example, through which racialized messages are received and processed? Moreover, are there differences that play a part in one's ability to resist negative messaging? Because individuals vary in the level of influence, it may be useful to determine any differences that create greater resilience in some versus others. Understanding this might assist in identifying interventions that may help others withstand these effects.

Race and racialization are not phenomena that affect only African American people. Cross-culturally, Black people within the African Diaspora, as well as non-Black people of color and White people, have experiences not only with race but also with anti-Blackness and anti-Black racialization processes. Future studies that capture channels of sexiness and experiences of racialization through these other lenses would be useful to the academy; however, even more insightful to the present research might be studies that capture the ways that anti-Black racialization particularly affects other groups' experiences of sexuality and the erotic self. While sexualized racism is not solely an African American phenomenon, neither is anti-Blackness, even among ethnic groups who are used to experiencing the former. There is already evidence that anti-Blackness has a history in, for example, many Latinx and South Asian communities (Aja, Bustillo, & Wallace, 2014; Kim, 2007; Massey, 2009; Patel, 2016; Telles & Ortiz, 2011);[26][27][28][29][30] further research into its relationship to sexuality would represent a useful next level of analysis.

Conclusion

The present research was an attempt to establish a theoretical basis for considering racialized sexual experience among African American people. It is by no means a definitive work; however, what it has hopefully done is forge the beginnings of a transformative conversation for African American people, the African diaspora and the human sexuality field at large. The time has come to reconcile the historical intellectual and political treatment of African American people with regard to the issue of sexuality. May this work be used as a proper springboard for making long-term positive change.

Notes

1 Staples, R. (2006). *Exploring black sexuality*. Lanham, MD: Rowan & Littlefield.
2 Staples (2006).
3 Weeks, J. (1985). *Sexuality and its discontents*. New York: Routledge.
4 Carrera, M. A. (1971). Preparation of a sex educator: A historical overview. *Family Coordinator*, 20(2), 99–108, 10p. https://doi.org/10.2307/581902
5 Sharma, A. (2010). Diseased race, racialized disease: The story of the Negro Project of the American Social Hygiene Association against the backdrop of the Tuskegee syphilis experiment. *Journal of African American Studies*, 14, 247–262. https://doi.org/10.1007/s12111-009-9099-0
6 Lewis, L. J. (2004). Examining sexual health discourses in a racial/ethnic context. *Archives of Sexual Behavior*, 33(3), 223–234. https://doi.org/10.1023/b:aseb.0000026622.31380.b4
7 Cunningham, E. C. (2010). Creation out of bounds: Toward wholistic identity. In Battle, J., & Barnes, S. L. (Eds.), *Black sexualities: Probing powers,*

passions, practices, and policies (Ch. 2). New Brunswick, NJ: Rutgers University Press.

8 Johnson, E. P. (2005). "Quare" studies, or (almost) everything I know about queer studies I learned from my grandmother. In Johnson, E. P., & Henderson, M. G. (Eds.), *Black queer studies: A critical anthology*. Durham, NC: Duke University Press.

9 Johnson (2005).

10 Johnson, E. P. (2003). *Appropriating blackness: Performance and the politics of authenticity*. Durham, NC: Duke University Press.

11 Goldfarb, E. (2009). A crisis of identity in sexuality education in America: How did we get here and where are we going? In Schroeder, E., & Kuriansky, J. (Eds.), *Sexuality education: Past, present, and future* (Vol. 1, Ch. 2). Westport, CT: Praeger.

12 Schroeder, E. (2009). The future of sexuality education in the twenty-first century and beyond. In Schroeder, E., & Kuriansky, J. (Eds.), *Sexuality education: Past, present, and future* (Vol. 1, Ch. 13). Westport, CT: Praeger.

13 Schroeder (2009).

14 Connell, C., & Elliott, S. (2009). Beyond the birds and the bees: Learning inequality through sexuality education. *American Journal of Sexuality Education*, 4(2), 83–102. https://doi.org/10.1080/15546120903001332

15 Hardy, K., & Laszloffy, T. A. (2002). Couple therapy using a multicultural perspective. In Gurman, A., & Jacobson, N. (Eds.), *Clinical handbook of couple therapy*. New York City: Guilford Press. Retrieved from www.researchgate.net/profile/Tracey_Laszloffy/publication/232486494_Couple_therapy_using_a_multicultural_perspective/links/546df10e0cf2d5ae3670c67a.pdf

16 Hardy & Laszloffy (2002).

17 Hardy & Laszloffy (2002).

18 Tuckwell, G. (2002). *Racial identity, white counsellors and therapists*. Buckingham: Open University Press.

19 Moodley, R., Lago, C., & Talahite, A. (Eds.). (2004). *Carl Rogers counsels a black client: Race and culture in person-centered counseling*. Ross-on-Wye: PCCS Books.

20 Jackson, C. (2018). Why we need to talk about race. *Therapy Today*, 29(8), 8–13.

21 McKenzie-Mavinga, I. (2018). Addressing racism in therapeutic practice: Isha McKenzie-Mavinga explores the powerful forces that prevent racism being discussed in therapy. *Therapy Today*, 29(8), 36–39.

22 Strean, M. (1983). *The sexual dimension: A guide for the helping professional.* New York: The Free Press.
23 Morris, M. W., Leung, K., Ames, D., & Lickel, B. (1999). Views from inside and outside: Integrating emic and etic insights about culture and justice judgment. *Academy of Management Review, 24*(4), 781–796. https://doi.org/10.5465/amr.1999.2553253
24 Rajack-Talley, T. A., Smith, S. E., Best, L., Della, L. J., D'Silva, M. U., Potter, D. A., & Carthan, Q. (2017). Epistemological inclusiveness in researching the African American community. *International Journal of Social Research Methodology, 20*(4), 411–423. https://doi.org/10.1080/13645579.2016.1187460
25 Rajack-Talley, et al. (2017).
26 Aja, A., Bustillo, D., & Wallace, A. (2014). Countering "anti-blackness" through "black-brown" alliances and inter-group coalitions: Policy proposals to "break the silence". *Journal of Intergroup Relations, 35*(2), 58–57. Retrieved from www.iaohra.org/index.htm
27 Kim, N. Y. (2007) Critical thoughts on Asian American assimilation in the whitening literature. *Social Forces, 86*(2), 561–574. Retrieved from http://nadiakimacademic.net/wp-content/uploads/2009/09/gallagher-SF-paper-Kim1.pdf
28 Massey, D. S. (2009). Racial formation in theory and practice: The case of Mexicans in the United States. *Race and Social Problems, 1*, 12–26. https://doi.org/10.1007/s12552-009-9005-3
29 Patel, S. (2016). Complicating the tale of "two Indians": Mapping "south Asian" complicity in white settler colonialism along the axes of caste and anti-blackness. *Theory & Event, 19*(4), 4–4. Retrieved from https://muse.jhu.edu/
30 Telles, E. E., & Ortiz, V. (2011). Racialization and Mexican incorporation: A reply to Lawrence Bobo and Jose Itzigsohn. *Du Bois Review, 8*(2), 506–510. https://doi.org/10.1017/s1742058x11000464

References

Aja, A., Bustillo, D., & Wallace, A. (2014). Countering "anti-blackness" through "black-brown" alliances and inter-group coalitions: Policy proposals to "break the silence". *Journal of Intergroup Relations, 35*(2), 58–57. Retrieved from www.iaohra.org/index.htm

Battle, J., & Barnes, S. L. (Eds.). (2005). *Black sexualities: Probing powers, passions, practices, and policies*. New Brunswick, NJ: Rutgers University Press.

Booth, B. (2014). *Toward sexual well-being: A grounded theory study of the lived experience of sexuality*. Unpublished doctoral dissertation, Widener University.

Breuss, C., & Greenberg, J. (2009). *Sexuality education: Theory and practice*. Sudbury, MA: Jones and Bartlett Publishers.

Bullough, V. (1994). *Science in the bedroom: A history of sex research*. New York: Basic Books.

Carrera, M. A. (1971). Preparation of a sex educator: A historical overview. *Family Coordinator, 20*(2), 99–108, 10p. https://doi.org/10.2307/581902

Connell, C., & Elliott, S. (2009). Beyond the birds and the bees: Learning inequality through sexuality education. *American Journal of Sexuality Education, 4*(2), 83–102. https://doi.org/10.1080/15546120903001332

Cooper, B. (2018). *Eloquent rage*. New York: St. Martin's Press.

Cunningham, E. C. (2010). Creation out of bounds: Toward wholistic identity. In Battle, J., & Barnes, S. L. (Eds.), *Black sexualities: Probing powers, passions, practices, and policies* (Ch. 2). New Brunswick, NJ: Rutgers University Press.

Duffy, J. (1990). *The sanitarians: A history of American public health*. Urbana, IL: University of Illinois Press.

Evans, M. W. (2010). Basic concepts in public health. In Haneline, M. R., & Meeker, W. C. (Eds.), *Introduction to public health for chiropractors* (Ch. 2). Burlington, MA: Jones & Bartlett Learning.

Frazier, E. F. (1948). Ethnic family patterns: The Negro family in the United States. *American Journal of Sociology, 53*(6), 435–438. https://doi.org/10.1086/220236

Goldfarb, E. (2009). A crisis of identity in sexuality education in America: How did we get here and where are we going? In Schroeder, E., & Kuriansky, J. (Eds.), *Sexuality education: Past, present, and future* (Vol. 1, Ch. 2). Westport, CT: Praeger.

Hardy, K., & Laszloffy, T. A. (2002). Couple therapy using a multicultural perspective. In Gurman, A., & Jacobson, N. (Eds.), *Clinical handbook of couple therapy*. New York City: Guilford Press. Retrieved from www.researchgate.net/profile/Tracey_Laszloffy/publication/232486494_Couple_therapy_using_a_multicultural_perspective/links/546df10e0cf2d5ae3670c67a.pdf

Ivanski, C., & Kohut, T. (2017). Exploring definitions of sex positivity through thematic analysis. *The Canadian Journal of Human Sexuality, 26*(3), 216–225. https://doi.org/10.3138/cjhs.2017-0017

Jackson, C. (2018). Why we need to talk about race. *Therapy Today, 29*(8), 8–13.

Johnson, E. P. (2003). *Appropriating blackness: Performance and the politics of authenticity.* Durham, NC: Duke University Press.

Johnson, E. P. (2005). "Quare" studies, or (almost) everything I know about queer studies I learned from my grandmother. In Johnson, E. P., & Henderson, M. G. (Eds.), *Black queer studies: A critical anthology.* Durham, NC: Duke University Press.

Johnson, E. P., & Henderson, M. G. (2005). Introduction: Queering black studies/ "Quaring" queer studies. In Johnson, E. P., & Henderson, M. G. (Eds.), *Black queer studies: A critical anthology.* Durham, NC: Duke University Press.

Kim, N. Y. (2007). Critical thoughts on Asian American assimilation in the whitening literature. *Social Forces, 86*(2), 561–574. Retrieved from http://nadiakimacademic.net/wp-content/uploads/2009/09/gallagher-SF-paper-Kim1.pdf

Lewis, L. J. (2004). Examining sexual health discourses in a racial/ethnic context. *Archives of Sexual Behavior, 33*(3), 223–234. https://doi.org/10.1023/b:aseb.0000026622.31380.b4

Martinson, F. M. (1994). *The sexual life of children.* Westport, CT: Bergin & Garvey.

Massey, D. S. (2009). Racial formation in theory and practice: The case of Mexicans in the United States. *Race and Social Problems, 1,* 12–26. https://doi.org/10.1007/s12552-009-9005-3

McBride, D. A. (2005). Straight black studies: On African American studies, James Baldwin, and Black Queer Studies. In Johnson, E. P., & Henderson, M. G. (Eds.), *Black queer studies: A critical anthology.* Durham, NC: Duke University Press.

McKenzie-Mavinga, I. (2018). Addressing racism in therapeutic practice: Isha McKenzie-Mavinga explores the powerful forces that prevent racism being discussed in therapy. *Therapy Today, 29*(8), 36–39.

Moodley, R., Lago, C., & Talahite, A. (Eds.). (2004). *Carl Rogers counsels a black client: Race and culture in person-centered counseling.* Ross-on-Wye: PCCS Books.

Morris, M. W., Leung, K., Ames, D., & Lickel, B. (1999). Views from inside and outside: Integrating emic and etic insights about culture and justice judgment. *Academy of Management Review*, 24(4), 781–796. https://doi.org/10.5465/amr.1999.2553253

Moynihan, D. P. (1965). *The Negro family: The case for national action*. Washington, DC: United States Department of Labor.

Patel, S. (2016). Complicating the tale of "two Indians": Mapping "south Asian" complicity in white settler colonialism along the axes of caste and anti-blackness. *Theory & Event*, 19(4), 4–4. Retrieved from https://muse.jhu.edu/

Rajack-Talley, T. A., Smith, S. E., Best, L., Della, L. J., D'Silva, M. U., Potter, D. A., & Carthan, Q. (2017). Epistemological inclusiveness in researching the African American community. *International Journal of Social Research Methodology*, 20(4), 411–423. https://doi.org/10.1080/13645579.2016.1187460

Rosen, G. (1958). *A history of public health*. Baltimore, MD: Johns Hopkins University Press.

Schroeder, E. (2009). The future of sexuality education in the twenty-first century and beyond. In Schroeder, E., & Kuriansky, J. (Eds.), *Sexuality education: Past, present, and future* (Vol. 1, Ch. 13). Westport, CT: Praeger.

Sharma, A. (2010). Diseased race, racialized disease: The story of the Negro Project of the American Social Hygiene Association against the backdrop of the Tuskegee syphilis experiment. *Journal of African American Studies*, 14, 247–262. https://doi.org/10.1007/s12111-009-9099-0

Sithole, T. (2016). The concept of the black subject in Fanon. *Journal of Black Studies*, 47(1), 24–40. https://doi.org/10.1177/0021934715609913

Snorton, C. R. (2014). *Nobody is supposed to know; Black sexuality on the down low*. Minneapolis, MN: University of Minnesota Press. https://doi.org/10.5749/minnesota/9780816677962.001.0001

Staples, R. (2006). *Exploring black sexuality*. Lanham, MD: Rowan & Littlefield.

Stephens, D. P., & Phillips, L. D. (2003). Freaks, gold diggers, divas, and dykes: The sociohistorical development of adolescent African American women's sexual scripts. *Sexuality & Culture*, 7(Winter), 3–49. https://doi.org/10.1007/bf03159848

Strean, M. (1983). *The sexual dimension: A guide for the helping professional*. New York: The Free Press.

Telles, E. E., & Ortiz, V. (2011). Racialization and Mexican incorporation: A reply to Lawrence Bobo and Jose Itzigsohn. *Du Bois Review*, 8(2), 506–510. https://doi.org/10.1017/s1742058x11000464

Tuckwell, G. (2002). *Racial identity, white counsellors and therapists*. Buckingham: Open University Press.

Weeks, J. (1985). *Sexuality and its discontents*. New York: Routledge.

Wilson, T. O. (2016). HIV criminalization: A continuation of racial-sexual terror exacted on the bodies of black msm. In Nix-Stevenson, D., Miller, P. C., & Brock, R.(Eds.), *Critical Black studies reader*. Oxford: Peter Lang Publishers, Inc. https://doi.org/10.3726/978-1-4539-1896-8

Woo, G. W., Soon, R., Thomas, M. S., & Kaneshiro, B. (2011). Factors affecting sex education in the school system. *Journal of Pediatric Adolescent Gynecology, 24*, 142–146. https://doi.org/10.1016/j.jpag.2010.12.005

Yancy, G. (2008). *Black bodies, white gazes*. Lanham, MD: Rowman & Littlefield Publishers.

AFTERWORD

It has been just under five years since the first batch of data for this study was collected. In that time I have given several different presentations on my findings at various conferences, including but not limited to the 2018 Annual Meeting of the American Association of Sexuality Educators, Counselors and Therapists; the 2018 Woodhull Sexual Freedom Summit; the 2019 American Sociological Association; the 2019 SSSS Annual Meeting; and the 2019 World Association for Sexual Health Conference, held in Mexico City. Ironically, it was at the 2019 AASECT Annual Meeting in Philadelphia where I was first offered the opportunity to turn my ideas into a book. Though I am not entirely sure who made the initial introduction to Clare Ashworth of Taylor & Francis on my behalf (my guess is that it might have been Bill Taverner of the Center for Sex Education, though I apologize if I've gotten that incorrect, as it is quite possible), I extend my eternal gratitude to whomever perceived me worthy enough to make that initial inquiry.

In June 2020, I was invited by educator, consultant and "Unprofessional Professional" Stephanie Zapata to share my thoughts in a 90-minute workshop for the inaugural Sexuality Liberators and Movers (S.L.A.M.) Virtual Conference. Beyond the sheer grandness of the event in and of itself (particularly while in the midst of, arguably, the second greatest pandemic in contemporary human history after HIV/AIDS), I remain awed and humbled by what that opportunity allowed me to conceptualize as a potential way forward for our profession. In the following paragraphs, I would like to share a few excerpts from the transcript of that presentation ("From Theory to Practice: Abolishing Anti-Blackness From the Sex Education Classroom"), which I hope can further drive home the very real challenges and practical opportunities that addressing racialization through sex ed provide to sexuality practitioners.

Excerpts From "From Theory to Practice: Abolishing Anti-Blackness From the Sex Education Classroom"

Good Morning, and welcome to this first workshop session of the S.L.A.M. Conference: From Theory to Practice: Abolishing Anti-Blackness From the Sex Education Classroom. Thank you so much for choosing to be part of this session. My name is Tracie Gilbert, and I have the great pleasure of being your facilitator for this morning.

There are a few assumptions you can make about the ideas I'm sharing with you today, which are based on both my professional expertise and what I know to be true about social knowledge creation in general. While my ideas do have universal applicability, they have always centered on and WILL always center on the lived experience of African American people, as that is what I know most. In addition, the vast majority of my professional experience has been with adolescent populations—most specifically middle- through college-aged young people, which is why I will be talking often about sex ed within a K-12 setting. At the same time, I am aware that these ideas are socially constructed and are open to negotiation as other Black scholars add their particular enhancements to them. Notice that I specify "BLACK" scholars, in terms of the particular folks I am open to having [make adjustments to] my work. Those of you who are not Black are welcome to consider how this work might be used to enhance any work you're doing with both Black and non-Black populations; however, I am not at all interested in your particular critiques, so I will ask that you keep them to yourself.

For those who are currently working with young people in a formal or regulated capacity—meaning that you are funded by a government agency that is looking to do targeted work around HIV or pregnancy prevention—I want to offer this note of full transparency: I don't anticipate my ideas being ones that you will be able to implement fully, particularly if you are committed to using an evidence-based intervention. After taking some time to reflect on the thoughts I've shared, I encourage you to consider having some intentional conversations with both yourself and your colleagues about whether a truly liberating sex education for Black people is something you can provide and to be forthright with any truths that come up for you during that process.

So let's get into this a little bit more and think about what's specifically missing. To this end, I want to begin by bringing in the most quintessential debate we've based this field on, specifically that of whether we should be using "Abstinence-Only" or "Comprehensive" in our sex ed. Let's begin there and see where we go.

If you consider the Abstinence-Only versus Comprehensive debate in and of itself, in an ideal world where race is not actually a thing, then I think you've got a useful foundation to at least begin thinking about the topic of sexual liberation. HOWEVER . . . if we are AT ALL considering the role of history and social construction in shaping the sex ed discourse, then we need to consider that this debate by itself is incomplete. To begin looking at the full picture we have to acknowledge that everything we understand about what's most moral or healthy or safe or "best practice" in sexuality and sexual knowledge has been based on an ideal of Whiteness and most often on the backs of Black and Brown, but especially Black, people. This means that, by and large, Black people have never had the full-scale agency to define the parameters of sexual health and wellness—or even sexual knowledge—for themselves outside of these lenses.

Both camps have essentialized what it means to be sexual and sexually active such that prevention becomes the only best option asserted within each. While this is not as much the case with Abstinence-Only, I would argue, since the goal is often more morally than medically focused, both camps still see sexual health as medicalized and administered from the outside. And at the end of the day, even if we were to value each of these perspectives equally as sex ed strategies, we have still not addressed the question of anti-Blackness and how it has affected Black people's ability to even enter this debate on an even keel with other groups. So there's the setup, if that makes sense to folks.

I want you also to think about the role of a person's worldview in shaping what they know to be true about how the world works versus what others with different worldviews know to be true. Psychologist Kobi Kambon suggests that, in the case of the "big C" cultural worldview, there are fundamental differences between how European societies (and those that have been socialized under them) see and treat the world and how folks who have been socialized under African-Centered philosophies see and treat it. In terms of cosmology, Kambon argues that the Eurocentric perception of reality centers on the idea of there being extreme independence or separateness between beings, whereas Afrocentric cosmology centers on a belief in the inextricable interdependence of all things—not just people but ideas and ideologies as well—essentially, the "both/and." Ontologically, Kambon argues that Eurocentric thinking centers on the material and, basically, the idea that what you see is what you get and that when you die that's all there ever was. From an Africentric perspective, however, Kambon suggests that there is not only material reality but also spiritual reality that exists not just within the body but beyond the body as well and beyond even time and space.

When thinking of epistemology—again, how we know what we know—Kambon argues that the Western world prioritizes cognition and how strong we perceive our brains to be. For example, if you know the quote "I think, therefore I am," that's where that comes in. From an Africentric perspective, however, knowledge is gained as much through our intuition as it is through our cognition such that a person can know what they know without having studied someone or something else to get there. Finally, when we compare Eurocentric versus Africentric axiologies, Kambon argues that even more conflict exists there, between the former framework that prioritizes a person–object relationship, to the level of dominance (i.e., objectification) and the latter that prioritizes collaboration and relationship—where there might be some healthy competition between people however, at the end of the day, connection is deemed most important because everyone is cared for and their basic humanity is valued.

In looking at this list cumulatively, I encourage you to consider how sex ed in the present day is ABSOLUTELY informed by a Eurocentric worldview. And you might not see it that way; however, when we think about how sex ed is usually done, consider that, in most cases, young people are taken away from their communities and placed with other individual students in their classrooms, maybe needlessly separated from each other by gender and in some cases under the guise of convincing parents to trust us without always knowing what we will or won't discuss or even if we know more than they do. In our classrooms the lessons that young people are given center on assumed "concrete," material knowledge: contraceptive types, exact names of body parts, hard and fast rules about sexual identity labels, gender identities, etc. It's assumed that one has sexual knowledge when they can demonstrate what they know versus what they believe or have conceived for themselves. And at the end of the day, sexuality becomes a type of production that is assumed to be best when self-definitive, outside facing and out loud, having nothing to do with anyone other than the individual themselves. Now, to be 100% CLEAR: this is not AT ALL to paint Eurocentric thinking as automatically all bad and Afrocentric thinking as automatically all good. That said, when we lift up and center Eurocentric models of education in sex ed, we are not doing all we can to effectively address gaps that are clearly present for the people in our classroom spaces. So what's the alternative?

Well, this is actually where an African-Centered Educational Philosophy comes in. This is a framework that was created by psychologist Na'im Akbar, whose work has centered for years on African American psychological experiences. This is not the only model of African-centered philosophy that exists in the world; however, I think it's one of the few that could apply both to general knowledge and sexuality education. When we think of the aim of traditional sex ed, as I've mentioned, the goal is often some attainment of sexuality or sexual health that may or may not represent the individual's authentic reality. When incorporating an ACE Philosophy, however, the goal is less about being someone else and more about mastering one's self and the particularities of one's unique environment. For example, an ACE sex ed classroom might talk about not only various types of contraceptive methods but also the history of the reproductive justice movement in the U.S. or the indigenous roots of many of the hormonal methods on the market today.

From an ACE perspective, discussions of consent would not only include sex but also consider how conversations about consent can be used to push back against hyper-disciplinary school environments, overcontrolling loved ones or police patrols. So ACE really takes a comprehensive discourse to a whole other level by factoring in the full extent of the student's life and how sexuality interacts with other systems. And when the markers of sexual intelligence are measured, they are less about what the learner can recite and more about how they have made active use of what they've learned and grown in their ability to think critically about that knowledge and make sound decisions that prepare them for a life of sexual wellness and wholeness.

So just to review briefly, the four intelligences within an African-Centered Epistemological Perspective are:

1. Knowledge of the collective and historical reality of self (knowing what you people have been through and continue to face);
2. Knowledge of the environmental obstacles to effective self-development;
3. Actions initiated to remove or master obstacles, which for me includes increasing one's capacity to know for sure that those obstacles can be removed or mastered; and
4. Knowledge of the Divine and universal laws that guide human development toward ultimate knowledge of the Creator.

Now, before anyone gets worked up too much about what is meant by "the Divine" and "the Creator," I want to stress that there's some flexibility that can be employed when helping young people understand this. Everyone's relationship to Spirit will be different; however, I do believe there is yet another framework that can come into play here and have practical use for facilitating awareness of both "Divine" knowledge and universal law in the sex ed classroom. Audre Lorde's "Uses of the Erotic" is one of the most fantastic essays I've ever read about the sexual energy that exists within each of us regardless of age, gender or background. To be clear, I'm not—as she wasn't—talking about pornographic energy, though there is a time and place for that in another context. What is being referred to is the creative life force that exists in all of us that can assist in helping us achieve our deepest desires and realities. The erotic, as Lorde describes it, is "a measure between the beginnings of our sense of self and the chaos of our strongest feelings. [The Erotic] is an internal sense of satisfaction to which, once we have experienced it, we know we can aspire. For having experienced the fullness of this depth of feeling and recognizing its power, in honor and self-respect we can require no less of ourselves." Now, when you listen to this, I know it's easy to just write this off as poetry without practical substance; however, in truth, what would it mean to take sex ed out of its traditional path and re-root it not just in pursuit of "health," or even pleasure, but in pursuit of wholesale life satisfaction? What would it mean to give young people permission to name what counts as personal power for them and to conceive of tangible steps to make that power real? This is something I encourage us to think about as we press on.

So when we get to the brass tacks of it all, what does an African-Centered Epistemological Approach TRULY look like in sex ed? I think this is an amazing question, and to answer it I want to give you five specific norms or rules that I believe can help us establish how to concretely move forward. Number One: An ACE approach in sex ed provides instruction that actively divests from anti-Blackness and ALL its derivatives, PERIOD. This means that right off the bat we are looking for and giving light to any biases that may be showing up in our classrooms. We're doing this by doing our own pre-work about ourselves, our agencies and the communities we serve, and we are doing this in the classroom by inviting our students to actualize and verbalize what sex and sexuality are to them as well as what specific significance they have in their lives. An ACE approach means we model as best we can what an all-inclusive classroom looks like by inviting and welcoming all intersectional experiences to be brought to the table and navigating them without judgment or policing.

It means we ACTIVELY use gender-neutral language when we discuss sexual topics and not just when we know someone in the room is trans, queer or gender non-conforming. We actively name racism and ability and immigration status and housing stability and homophobia and transphobia as real-time barriers to sexual fulfillment, and we help students strategize about how to realistically move past them. We center diversity as the norm in ALL topics, including those that seem universal to us when they aren't—like anatomy or whether or not to parent. We invite students to acknowledge when something we've said doesn't sit right with them from their frame of reference, and when appropriate we acknowledge how Eurocentricity or White supremacy has played a part in creating that discomfort in the first place. Finally, in NO WAY, SHAPE OR FORM WHATSOEVER DO WE CAST JUDGMENT ON OUR STUDENTS FOR HOW THEY SHOW UP TO OUR CLASSROOMS WITHOUT FIRST ESTABLISHING THE OPPORTUNITY FOR THEM TO FIND THEMSELVES IN WHAT WE'RE OFFERING. For many of our students—hell, for many of us—it has taken and may take a while to unlearn and relearn a new way to see and move about an African-Centered sexual reality. It is in no one's best interest to give up on a student if we feel they haven't gotten fast enough to where we think they should be.

Number Two: An active ACE approach resists the Eurocentric cosmology of relying on binaries to understand the world. Far too often sex ed attempts to paint sexuality and sexual health as this cut and dried, cookie cutter way of existence without acknowledging that it's not how most of US, let alone most of our students, move about the world and our sexual universe. I would argue that an ACE approach to sex ed is inherently queer in all senses of the word because it is not tied to any outcome outside of self-determination, which is essentially rooted in a both/and—both brain and body, both light and shadow, both cognition and emotion and so on. I would argue that an ACE approach allows space for students to sit with and navigate gray areas on their own terms, validating sexual phenomena as they are, either with all the labels we choose to place on them or without any, if that is what one chooses.

Third, an ACE approach is communal and recognizes not only the benefit of fostering community in the teaching of sex ed but also the necessity of doing so. And we do this for two reasons, the first being for students to actively accept that their well-being is directly tied to the assured well-being of others. Which is to say, for example, that I don't learn how not to rape or how to honor others' pronouns just so I can be more accepting of others or avoid breaking the law. I learn these ideas because I recognize how not doing so has hampered my own freedom and that learning about them helps me grow in my capacity to BE free and thus useful to myself and my community. A community axiology addresses the toxic sense of alienation that we know so many young people feel and socializes them to take more active responsibility for each other—particularly the parts of each other we know exist in ourselves. Second, the communal aspect of African-Centered Epistemology allows space to alleviate the binary that currently exists between student and teacher by allowing space for peers to share knowledge with each other as well as space for teachers to share knowledge with parents and extended family members and vice versa, particularly in the case of addressing racialized sexuality, which is generations deep.

So the goal, then, would be to facilitate, for example, a space where a child learns how to clock white fetishization of Black bodies in media and can do so with their mother, who is willing, and their cousin, who is willing, and their gay uncle, who might be hesitant but loves the child enough to hear things out, and so on and so on. To do anything less than this, in my estimation, is not only not liberating but is also bordering on the unethical. Now, this is not to say that collaborative learning must be a concurrent process since young people might still want their spaces to talk without adult interference. The whole point of what I'm saying is that we should question any motivation we might have to educate a student (especially a child) without being responsive to the communities and contexts they come from and the pervasiveness of bias and phobias that can be brought to light and healed.

Fourth, an African-Centered Epistemological perspective incorporates trauma-informed practices that engage both cognitive and affective work within the learning and encourage their adoption among students. If we know that, as the book title suggests, *The Body Keeps the Score* when it comes to trauma, then we also know that the body must be one of the main actors involved in the healing/liberation process. Which is to say, sex ed doesn't have to just exercise the brain or exercise the body mindlessly; it can and should include mind–body integration exercises to help students tap into how these experiences live inside their bodies and how they can be effectively addressed when they don't feel pleasurable or life-affirming. Helping young people—especially those whose bodies have been terrorized—learn how to increase their somatic intelligence and intuition is HUGE, particularly if it can be matched with other grounding and therapeutic practices.

On another note, knowing that community concealment and shame have been some of the effects of anti-Blackness for many African American people, validating their initial resistance to talking openly about sex while facilitating safe space for students to eventually open up without being judged is another practice that can lend itself to ultimate self- and communal healing—keeping in mind that in some cases, our students MAY NOT EVER open up to us, particularly if our agencies have had a bad reputation in the community we're entering or if our presence in that space represents privilege or discrimination that the community has learned to resist. It is never a student's responsibility to open up to you if they don't want to, so even if they NEVER do, that doesn't preclude the opportunity you have to KEEP trying and to keep exploring for yourself what might be necessary to ensure success in that educational space—even if, in some cases, that may mean you remove yourself and make space for facilitators that are a better fit.

Finally, an African-Centered Epistemological perspective is sure to reposition and develop the learner as the primary decision maker for sexual decisions related to their own lives. Now, I know this one is difficult for some of us to wrap our heads around, especially if we're working with elementary or middle school young people. And yet I still assert this point because doing so requires us to own up to the fact that, in many ways, we have not effectively prepared young people to make sound decisions for themselves in MOST ways, not just in terms of their sexuality. We have adultified so many young people—especially Black children—by giving them access to mature content and experiences while at the same time not giving them any tools to think through that material in a developmentally mature way. Particularly as we're coming to understand the importance of young people understanding and negotiating concepts like boundaries and consent, the sex ed classroom should be the very place where we're also teaching our students to cultivate desire—giving them the space to imagine and to aspire, to express their wants unapologetically, while also cultivating their ability to pursue their desires in life-affirming ways and validating the ups and downs all along the way. An ACE approach requires that we be forthright and intentional about this entire process.

And so, ultimately, when I'm talking about an African-Centered approach, I'm simultaneously talking about both a healing and a liberating approach. For the teachers in the room, I'm still talking KSA, or Knowledge, Skills and Attitude; however, I'm talking about an enhanced KSA, one that shifts away from prevention–priority models based on rote information and skill building that may never actually be used or needed to a developmental model based on self-knowledge, self-determination and agency-building. Instead of asking of ourselves what we want our young people to know, or even what THEY want to know, an ACE approach sets us up to think about, and help young people think about, who they want to become. That, to ME, is the critical healing and sexual liberation we all need.

Those who do not practice sexuality may find little of use in this section of the book; however, as I've previously noted, the notion of racialized sexuality carries far greater implications for understanding sexuality than the conceptual. Sexuality education is as much a function of how we are taught to view sex as it is what we are taught to view; as such, truly just and equitable sex ed must lead the way in shifting how new and old learners come to understand and effectively tease out the parts of racialization that do not serve the healthy sexual beings they desire to become, nor those they desire to engage with.

As our profession finally awakens to action around issues of racial injustice, equity and diversity, I believe we must open the door for voices that can effectively point the way to learning that is radical (i.e., aimed and ready to uproot), transformative and healing, understanding that racism is not only what happens to the physicality of Black bodies but also the mental colonization of them. Surface solutions will get us only so far; the changing of minds and hearts, while difficult, is a must for sex ed that is truly rooted in freedom and redemption. This afterword is a direct call to sexuality practitioners who are not only the front line of access to the general public but are also uniquely trained in the theories and other competencies relevant to their work that best position them to contemplate and enact new ways forward that prevent otherwise toxic frameworks from gaining new territory. I welcome all those truly interested in this agenda to further the much needed conversation and thought work.

APPENDICES

APPENDIX A: BSE RESEARCH STUDY METHODOLOGY

As was stated at several points in the book, the purpose of this research was to provide beginning speculative theory about the social construction of African American sexuality and sexual self-schema, including their baseline organizing structures, from a contemporary, racialized perspective. Specifically, it addressed the following research question: "what can grounded theory clarify about the social construction of sexuality and sexual self-schema among a sample of African Americans in the 21st century?" Given its theoretical roots in symbolic interactionism and intention toward theory development, I could find no greater or more effective methodological approach for enacting the type of study proposed here than grounded theory. Generally speaking, grounded theory refers to the systematic acquisition and testing of data from one's population of interest as a means to gain abstract understanding of the experience under study (Charmaz, 2006). In contrast to other qualitative research methods that rely on applying previously established constructs and theoretical frameworks, grounded theory proceeds with a primary emphasis on collecting rich empirical data and using them to explain to the researcher what their topic of interest is and how it should, in fact, be interpreted (Glaser & Strauss, 1999).

While I presented several theories in Chapter 1 relative to the historicity of racialization in America, I intentionally provided no additional speculation as to the meaning or organizational structure of race with regard to African Americans in the present day. Forgoing conjecture in this regard allowed my research population to lead both problem development and analysis through the revelation of data from their own, real-time lived experience (Glaser & Strauss, 1999). What ultimately developed from this process was *emergent* theory regarding contemporary normative African American sexuality. All population sampling, data collection and data analysis for this study served this aim.

Usefulness of Grounded Theory to Sexological Research on African Americans

While it would have arguably been easier to design a study using preestablished "Black sexuality" perspectives or to rely on more description-focused research designs, to do so would have fallen outside my original intention, perhaps even adding to the original anti-Blackness problem, because such research has been so historically problem-centric. Grounded theory is most useful in the ways it engenders population empowerment given that inherent within its methodology is active engagement with the voice and perspectives of the research population (Oktay, 2012). This aspect of the model ultimately makes study participants co-creators in knowledge formation and interpretation—a position not consistently held among non-European populations in sexological research of the past (Weeks, 1985). This, in many ways, sets this study within the realm of social justice research.

Solid, substantial grounded theory research has the potential to more effectively inform strategies for social change—directly connecting theory and practice in the ways its architects, Barney Glaser and Anselm Strauss, originally intended (Charmaz, 2005; Glaser & Strauss, 1999; Oktay, 2012). In addition, grounded theory can help add weight to already existing social justice concepts (e.g., hegemony) when the latter are subsequently used to affirm, and are affirmed by, relevant empirical data (Charmaz, 2005). Finally, Charmaz suggests that grounded theory can be used to directly articulate the structures and machinations of inequality—how they form, operate and thrive. As all of these points have particular relevance to this study, they were actively included in its process.

Research Design

To complete this study, I conducted 95 in-person video and audio-recorded interviews, each consisting of at least one but no more than two people at a time. Participants were solicited to participate on an individual basis; however, pair interviews were conducted in some cases with participants who felt more comfortable speaking in the presence of their friends or other peers. No participant was required to interview with others if they did not wish to. Saturation did appear to occur early on—at least within the first 30 interviews. No formal limits, however, were established on the number of people I would interview. It was important to me, from a social justice perspective, to allow for the inclusion of as many interested and diverse Black voices as possible. Including additional interviews after the 30th allowed for expansion to a national sample, accommodating for any potential regional biases in the original interview set and adding more depth to the final analysis.

To avoid researcher bias, I refrained from developing any units of analysis prior to my interviews other than my population title, "African Americans" and "Blackness," both of which were, by necessity, defined in Chapter 1. "Sexuality," though undefined, was also an original unit of analysis. As interviews proceeded, "sexiness" became an additional unit, as some participants identified conceptual distinctions between the two. While participants were encouraged to answer questions in any way they felt most comfortable, the final data set consisted of only transcribed words and drawn pictures. Despite the information collected relative to my posed theoretical framework, I made no assumptions about what information would be revealed to me by my sample. My goal and position as the researcher was to effectively integrate all conversations into one cohesive, speculative set of concepts about the phenomenon under study.

It became apparent early on that comprehensive memoing after each interview would not be a feasible practice given both the intensity of the interview schedule and amount of information shared in each interview. Instead, general notes were created based on particular ideas generated during the conversation, particularly if they appeared to depart from preceding interviews. These notes were journaled by hand and occasionally used to make general estimations about categories that might be expanded on or adjusted at later points. The final coding process consisted of two steps: writing and sorting memos of all primer sheets and then writing and sorting memos of participants' verbal responses. A total of two major and eight minor concepts emerged from the data during this process. I believe these collectively serve to paint a picture of African American sexual epistemology that is a unique departure from previously established ideas.

Sampling

Because this research was specifically focused on African Americans, it was necessary for me to limit my population sample in this regard. This included excluding individuals who may live in the United States and identify as Black or of African descent but either do not identify as African American or do not descend from individuals who may have been subjected to U.S.-specific forms of anti-Blackness.[1] Coincidentally, I did have several individuals who did not meet the qualifications express disappointment at not being able to participate in the study as well as several individuals who signed up to participate but revealed only Caribbean or West African ancestry during the course of our interview. Because these participants were well aware of study expectations and self-selected to continue participation, responses from these individuals were not discarded (further explanation of this was given in Chapter 7). While I set no specific quotas, I set out to have as diverse a range of African American people as possible, as Sitron and Dyson (2012) note that such factors can diversify an otherwise similar population's sexual identity and experience. The ultimate sample (as shown in Table 1) consisted of African Americans from a wide range of ages, genders, sexual orientations and educational backgrounds. While these specific questions were not asked, additional sample diversity surfaced among the population relative to religious background, reading comprehension level, socioeconomic status, physical ability and physical and mental health status.

Participants for this study were recruited using a Study Interest Form that was circulated through word of mouth and email listserv posts and included as a scannable QR code on fliers posted at preapproved health centers and social service agencies in my local area. Because I was aware of intra-cultural dynamics that may exist around gender and sexual orientation, lending themselves to additional intersectional variations in the phenomenon under

Table 1 Participant Demographics

Criterion	Variability	Number of Recruited Participants
Age	18–20	4
	21–24	12
	25–29	24
	30–34	17
	35–39	18
	40–44	7
	45–49	4
	50–54	3
	55–59	1
	60+	2
Sexual Orientation	Asexual	1*
	Heterosexual	54
	Homosexual	5
	Bisexual	7
	Pansexual	6
	Polysexual	0
	Queer	14
	Other (Please Specify)	6
Gender Identity	Male	15
	Female	72
	Bigender	0
	Transgender	2
	Genderqueer/Gender Non-Conforming	3
	Other (Please Specify)	3

(*Continued*)

Table 1 (Continued)

Criterion	Variability	Number of Recruited Participants
Highest Degree Attained	No Schooling Completed	0
	High School Diploma	15
	Associate Degree	6
	Bachelor's Degree (BA, AB, BS)	28
	Master's Degree (MA, MS, MEng, MEd, MSW, MBA)	34
	Professional Degree (MD, DDS, DVM, LLB, JD)	3
	Doctorate Degree (PhD, EdD)	2
	Other (Please Specify)	4
	Did Not Answer	1
Location Born	Northeast	33
	Midwest	22
	South	27
	West	5
	Pacific (AK, HI)	1
	Other U.S. Territory	0
	Outside of U.S.	4
	Did Not Complete	1
Location Currently Residing	Northeast	38
	Midwest	18
	South	38
	West	0
	Pacific (AK, HI)	0
	Other U.S. Territory	0
	Outside of U.S.	0
	Did Not Answer	1

study (Brown Douglas, 1999; Collins, 2005), I conducted more targeted recruitment of LGBTQ individuals by reaching out to African American LGBT-serving organizations as well. Over the course of the study, it became apparent that more targeted recruitment would be needed among men and male-identified individuals as well. Several study announcements were posted in social media groups that were particularly male-centered or predominantly male in membership (e.g., Facebook Fathers clubs). In addition, I made specific requests of African American male-identified people I knew, requesting help with increasing participation in the study and helping to spread the word to other African American male-identified people.

Ultimately, advertisements circulated through social media were the most successful form of sample generation, particularly those sent through Facebook, Twitter and Meetup. Response to the study was overwhelmingly positive, with individuals eagerly making contact with me from throughout the United States and at least two other parts of the world. Most engagement with the study was two-fold: interested people both signed up for the study and shared the study announcement with their respective social networks. In other cases, individuals with large social media platforms (accounts with 10,000+ followers) reposted my original study announcement, inspiring others to sign up through indirect endorsement. In a third set of cases, individuals personally contacted peers they believed would be interested in participating in the study, encouraged them to sign up and helped to coordinate interview spaces for me to meet with interested people in their respective areas. A total of 238 people completed the initial Study Interest Form; the final sample size represents those with whom I was able to coordinate interviews within immediate time and travel constraints. Outside of initial requirements that participants be African American and 18 years of age, all participants were English-speaking, able to give some thought to the concept of sex/sexuality and willing to participate in an in-person interview. For their participation in the study, respondents were entered into a drawing, the winner of which received their choice of $50 personally or a $100 donation to the charity of their choice.

Data Collection and Analysis

Data collection for this study was completed via in-person written and conversational interviews. Two hours were scheduled for completion of each interview; average conversations lasted between 30 and 45 minutes.

Most interviews were conducted in publicly accessible spaces, specifically in professional co-working offices and lounge areas, as available. When adequate co-working space could not be secured, interviews were held in domestic rental spaces, including hotel rooms and AirBNB locations. Interviewees were invited to suggest places that would be conducive to conversation as well; as such, interviews were also conducted at interviewee's own professional office spaces or apartment community rooms. Public businesses such as coffee shops and restaurants were expressly avoided to prevent any potential legal disputes around logos, signage, licensed decor, etc., showing up on tape. Reasonable accommodations were made to work with the particular needs of all interviewees; overall, most participants expressed comfort with the arrangements made and were eager to accommodate me as the researcher as well.

While most of the interviews conducted were one on one, two interviews were conducted with two individuals simultaneously per their request. The purpose of offering both group and one-on-one interview options was three-fold: a) to facilitate and observe any nonverbal negotiations that may be exhibited regarding shared understanding of concepts, b) to allow participants space to maximize their comfort level in engaging with the topic and c) to facilitate participant leadership in knowledge creation around the research question. Each interview was preceded by a brief overview of the Study Consent Form (Appendix C), which included all study expectations, caveats and benefits. Participants were given two copies of the consent form to sign, after which they were given a Study Demographic Form to complete (Appendix D). Each participant received a copy of the consent form signed by both them and myself; I kept the second copy for my own records. Once the demographic form was completed, the official interview commenced.

To remain open to the full extent of grounded theory methodology, I could not begin the interview with an extensive preliminary set of questions. Instead, I selected two major interview questions about sexuality and race and then added clarifying questions as needed in response to specific information provided by each participant (see Interview Schedule, Appendix E). Previous researchers have noted the intellectual challenge of asking the general populace to talk about their own sexuality (Booth, 2014; Sitron & Dyson, 2003). I, too, found similar yet divergent challenges among my sample in speaking directly about sexuality, and this is discussed further in the next section. Even with this barrier, it was important for me to select effective "spiller" questions for the conversation—questions general enough to be conceptually accessible to a wide range of people, provocative enough to yield substantial data and relevant enough to be capable of addressing the overarching research topic (Nathaniel, 2008). After giving it considerable thought, I settled on first asking, "What is sexiness to you?" I chose this question for two reasons, the first being because I believed "sexiness" to be a ubiquitous concept to which many people had likely been exposed in one form or another prior to the conversation. Second, I believed the suffix -ness, when interpreted etymologically as the state or condition of a thing (-ness, n.d.), had enough conceptual equivalence to the suffix in sexuality, -ity, also meaning quality or state of (-ity, n.d.), to elicit information for relevant analysis even if participants were unaware of said connections prior to our meeting. This choice would ultimately serve me well, as participants were consistently eager to answer the question or discuss various reservations they had in doing so.

To increase participant reflection and solicit various forms of response, I also opted to open each interview using a "primer sheet"—an otherwise blank sheet of paper featuring the opening research question. Participants were provided the sheet with an array of pens, markers, crayons and colored pencils and then instructed to respond to the question in whatever way felt authentic to them. No time limit was given for completion of the primer sheet. Once participants completed the sheet, I asked them to explain their motivation for what they wrote or drew along with any underlying symbolic meaning, their perceived understanding of the relationship between the concepts on their sheet and sexuality and how they saw themselves fitting into that same ideology. One of my earliest respondents did appear to get tripped up over the questions; others remarked how they had never been asked such questions before or even considered them for themselves. Over time, I chose to add verbiage to my initial welcome monologue, encouraging participants not to worry about "giving the right answer," as many articulated their desire to do so. That said, most individuals ultimately exhibited comfort while answering the follow-up questions or appeared to loosen up after the additional reassurance was offered. Both the contents of the primer sheet and subsequent discussion were included in the data analysis.

My second major question, "How does being Black factor into sexiness?" did not prove to be as initially effective as I'd wished in stimulating dialogue. In hindsight, I realized the question was inherently assumptive in nature. Adjusting the question to "Does being Black affect the way you think about and/or experience sex? And if so, how?" triggered an almost instantaneous shift in the level and extent of participant response, with almost every single following participant responding lucidly to the question. In later interviews, I added the follow-up question "Does being Black affect the way you think about yourself as a sexual being?" Again, participants appeared to have no difficulty in understanding the question and provided substantial information in response.

An additional observation I found during interviews involved some participants using the starter question to discuss what was "sexy" to them versus what might be considered "sexiness" as I attempted to capture it. Etymologically speaking, asking "What is sexy to you?" is on par with sexiness and sexuality as noted earlier; however, I was concerned that, given social convention regarding the specific word, discussing "sexy" might skew participant responses more toward a specific set of ideas deemed sexually attractive by society and not necessarily ideas that were authentic to their own lives. As was also noted by several participants, what one might consider sexually attractive is not entirely the same as what one might consider sexual or the "nature" or essence of sexuality.

Finally, in the instance that someone did identify something considered sexy, I was aware that said identification might also prove more figurative than literal. For example, a response of "car" as sexy or sexiness may represent its literal presence in one's conceptualization of sexuality or it may, as was the case with several participants, represent other concepts—for example, femininity or sophistication. The primer sheet follow-up questions I used served as a solid safeguard against ambiguity in this regard. The two that specifically helped were a) "Is there anything on your sheet that is more figurative or symbolic than literal?" and b) "Do you feel that what you've written on your sheet is a good description of the concept of sexuality when it shows up in your mind?" Answers participants gave to this question added greatly to refining the emergent theory.

As noted, all conversations were audio- and video-recorded;[2] video recording was a required part of the interview, the rationale for which was provided to participants during the informed consent process. In line with basic ethical standards regarding informed consent, participants were notified of all research parameters prior to soliciting their commitment to participate. Participants were given the option to leave the study at any point and provided a list of resources for accessing mental health support for any discomfort that might have surfaced during the process (see Appendix F). Though no such feelings were expressed, participants were made aware that such discomfort was possible prior to securing their consent. Coding and conceptualizing of theory began with the first interview and proceeded well past a clear saturation point for my theory's core concepts. To reach emergent theory, I used Glaser and Strauss's (1999) four overlapping stages of comparative analysis, which are briefly described in the following sections.

Comparing Incidents Applicable to Each Theoretical Category

As responses and observations (labeled "incidents") were recorded, they were coded into conceptual groups that seemed appropriately related. Given the intensity of the interview schedule, most incidents were recorded mentally or via journal and then officially coded and sorted at the end of the data collection process. All primer sheets were coded first using an axial coding method centered on the original conceptual framework of "sexiness." Approximately 700 codes were created from the sheets, which included literal words written by each respondent and basic descriptions (e.g., body, candle) of visual images. As each new incident was coded, it was simultaneously added to like incidents provided by other respondents and then compared with other sets of like incidences until ultimately being combined into particular comparative groups. The comparison process is what allowed me to generate constitutive categories of the "sexiness" concept and their properties (e.g., essential characteristics, degrees of variation) as well as to speculate about relationships between the theoretical categories created (Glaser & Strauss, 1999). This second step, in which my initial analyses and ideas were logged and used to help strategize next research steps, is referred to as memoing (Strauss & Corbin, 1998). Codes from both the primer sheets and subsequent interview questions were transcribed by hand using 3 × 5-inch index cards. Categories were given names and descriptions based on the most apparent common terms or characteristics identified within each physical pile of cards.

Integrating Categories and Their Properties

As my initial categories gained strength and dimension, newly recorded incidents—gained from reviewing each interview transcript—were compared with the qualities of each established category and no longer with other incidents themselves. This constant comparison process, as Glaser and Strauss (1999) noted, forged an integration of knowledge accumulated about these categories into conceptual relationships that encompassed their respective sub-parts. It was simultaneous theoretical sampling and analysis that allowed me to see the beginnings of emergent theory. By the time I began to review interviews for additional incidents and relevant quotes to explain them, what began as loosely articulated conjectures began to take on enough of a shape to constitute clearer, more articulable ideas (Glaser & Strauss, 1999). Review of participant explanations also allowed me to begin articulating potential working relationships between the categories (aka, creating theory).

Delimiting the Theory

Generally speaking, new information gathered during the delimiting process should be used primarily to add texture and dimension to the emergent theory and its properties. If any new changes are needed, they should be focused primarily on enhancing salient concept properties or, if necessary, removing extraneous tangents (Glaser & Strauss, 1999). While most of the information provided by respondents yielded very little tangency from initially established categories, what became clear in review of the interview transcripts was that the primer sheets could only, understandably, tell part of the story. Participants' explanations of the concepts they chose began to clarify which categories had legitimate meaning in and of themselves and which were more indicative of larger or different yet related ideas.

New engagement with the data regarding relationships between primer sheet responses and sexuality as a particular concept facilitated a sorting process whereby relationships between categories began to more clearly crystallize. Some became more centered, some became subsumed within others and others reorganized to the margins. Once it finally became clear what specific categories were taking shape in the emergent theory, ideas that did not appear to speak to the categories presented, introduce new categories for integration or provide a basis for establishing or explaining category relationships were ignored. Ultimately, the final set of concepts was a direct product of the reduction process, which allowed me to reorganize categories more easily in ways that covered more conceptual ground more parsimoniously.

From the perspective of some grounded theorists, once saturation is reached, new data cease to provide information that departs from what has already been uncovered (Glaser & Strauss, 1999; Oktay, 2012). Though data analysis did not proceed in the traditional way of the method, evidence from field notes and hindsight review of the progression of interviews revealed that theoretical saturation points were well reached in all core categories.

Assessing Data and Theory Quality

When the steps of grounded theory method are effectively employed, what is produced is theory that is clear, substantial and useful for explaining the desired phenomenon under study. While I would not suggest that this work represents definitive knowledge on this particular subject, I have done what I believe to be due diligence in producing such a theory. Data assessment has been a continuous process fulfilled through constant comparison of new data with preceding data, specifically examining consistencies or detours. In several cases, I reviewed data discursively with participants themselves, revisiting previous conversations with other interviewees for clarification or concept reinforcement when similar ideas appeared to be resurfacing in the moment. In other cases, I utilized a journal to record particular moments that stood out to me among respondents and that either appeared to add texture to a previous established theme or concept in the data or presented new ideas—along with new questions—to be considered in future interviews. Throughout the interview process, I developed several partial theories in my mind corresponding to the research question. To avoid running with my own unchecked bias on the relationship between emergent categories, however, I was sure to wait until comprehensive review of the primer sheets before attempting to crystallize categories into a credible conceptual foundation.

Evaluating the research process itself was an additional, indirect aspect of data assessment. Beyond being consistent in the data collection and analysis, I reviewed previous scholarship on the grounded theory method, including specific essays on effective memoing and theory delimitation (Kelle, 2007; Lempert, 2007). The resultant theory has been thoroughly delimited and appears to genuinely reflect respondents' expressed concerns and priorities with regard to the topic. Finally, the theory presented here was reviewed by the members of my dissertation committee, each of whom provided significant feedback that aided in the clarification of its principles and ideas. I will continue to hone the credibility of this theory through subsequent presentations and research of additional populations, including but not limited to other Black people within the African diaspora. It is my expectation that subsequent conversations and presentations of this theory will reveal and enhance its long-term strength and relevance.

Notes

1 The impetus to focus on "African Americans" versus "Blacks" is as much of a logistical choice as it is a definitional one. While it is my opinion and that of many others that sexualized anti-Blackness is a global phenomenon (see Costa Vargas, 2008, for example), contending with sexuality as it intersects with the diversity of Africans in the diaspora ultimately falls outside the scope of this particular study.
2 Though recording of interviews is discouraged in classical grounded theory, the proposed use of videotaping is purposeful as a means to capture relevant unspoken communication from participants and in light of the historical connections between anti-Blackness and African American bodies discussed extensively in Chapter 1.

References

Booth, B. (2014). *Toward sexual well-being: A grounded theory study of the lived experience of sexuality*. Unpublished doctoral dissertation, Widener University.

Brown Douglas, K. (1999). *Sexuality and the black church: A womanist perspective*. Maryknoll, NY: Orbis Books.

Charmaz, K. (2005). Grounded theory in the 21st century: Applications for advancing social justice studies. In Denzin, N. K., & Lincoln, Y. E. (Eds.), *Handbook of qualitative research* (3rd ed., pp. 507–535). Thousand Oaks, CA: Sage Publications. https://doi.org/10.1108/09504120610655394

Charmaz, K. (2006). *Constructing grounded theory: A practical guide through qualitative analysis.* Thousand Oaks, CA: Sage Publications.

Collins, P. H. (1990). *Black feminist thought: Knowledge, consciousness, and the politics of empowerment* (1st ed.). New York: Routledge.

Costa Vargas, J. H. (2008). *Never meant to survive: Genocide and utopias in black diaspora communities.* Lanham, MD: Rowman & Littlefield Publishers.

Glaser, B. G., & Strauss, A. L. (1999). *The discovery of grounded theory: Strategies for qualitative research* [Kindle Fire version]. New Brunswick, NJ: Transaction Publishers. https://doi.org/10.4324/9780203793206

-ity. (n.d.). *Merriam-Webster's collegiate dictionary online.* Retrieved from https://www.merriam-webster.com/dictionary/-ity.

Kelle, U. (2007). The development of categories: Different approaches in grounded theory. In Bryant, A., & Charmaz, K. (Eds.). *The SAGE handbook of grounded theory.* Los Angeles: Sage Publications.

Lempert, L. B. (2007). Asking question of the data: Memo writing in the grounded theory tradition. In Bryant, A., & Charmaz, K. (Eds.). *The SAGE handbook of grounded theory.* Los Angeles: Sage Publications.

Nathaniel, A. (2008). Eliciting spill: A methodological note. *Grounded Theory Review, 7*(1). Retrieved from http://groundedtheoryreview.com/2008/03/30/1063/.

-ness. (n.d.). *Merriam-Webster's online dictionary.* Retrieved from https://www.merriam-webster.com/dictionary/-ness.

Oktay, J. (2012). *Grounded theory.* New York: Oxford University Press.

Sitron, J. A. & Dyson, D. A. (2012). Validation of sexological worldview: A construct for use in the training of sexologists in sexual diversity. *Sage OPEN,* 1–16. Retrieved from http://sgo.sagepub.com/content/spsgo/early/2012/03/05/2158244012439072.full.pdf

Strauss, A. L., & Corbin, J. (1998). *Basics of qualitative research: Techniques and procedures for developing grounded theory* (2nd ed.). Thousand Oaks, CA: Sage Publications.

Weeks, J. (1985). *Sexuality and its discontents.* New York: Routledge.

APPENDIX B: INTERVIEW SCHEDULE

Part One: OPENING

A. Hello! I'm Tracie, and it's a pleasure to meet you! Thank you very much for taking time out to speak with me. We are here today to discuss the topic of sexuality. I will be asking you questions about your experiences and perspectives and will ask you to be as candid and open as you wish. Before we do that, however, there are a few items that need to be reviewed first.

- *Informed Consent Forms*: Before we begin, I must make sure that all participants complete an Informed Consent Form. This form is critical to making sure that you are fully aware of what this study consists of so that you are making an informed choice to participate.
- *Media Release Forms*: In addition to the Informed Consent Form, I am also asking that each participant complete a media release form, as these interviews will be videotaped, and that footage may be used in the future for special educational programming. You are absolutely

NOT required to consent to my using your footage in this way, and you can still participate in the study if you do not give me permission; however, completing this form will allow me to use it without further compensation to you. In either case, your participation is appreciated.

- *Demographic Survey*: Finally, I am asking that each participant take 3–5 minutes to complete a small demographic survey for this study. This survey will be used to help me gain clarity about who specifically among African Americans have been surveyed and any differences in perspective that may come up between respondents. Please answer each question noted here and let me know if you need anything explained.

B. Now that these items have been completed, let me say that I am excited to continue this discussion with you. I believe that you have information that is invaluable to what others and I do in the field of sexuality education. As we proceed, I would like to invite you to relax and get comfortable. This is a space where you can feel safe to answer the questions, and there's not anything you can tell me that will make me embarrassed or uncomfortable. I ask you to use as much candor and honesty as you wish. Do you have any final questions for me before we get started?

Part Two: PRIMER EXERCISE

Okay, now what I'd like to do is have you complete a small brainstorm-type exercise with the materials on the table. Using any of the materials here on the table, please take 5–7 minutes to answer the following question: what is "sexiness" to you?

Part Three: INTERVIEW (Note: this exact question used in the protocol will, by necessity, evolve over time as interview data are collected and more insight is gained regarding the most appropriate questions to ask.)	A. Sexuality • Okay, so tell me more about what's on your sheet. What made you put it there? • Are there aspects of what you put down that are more symbolic than literal? If so, what do they symbolize? • Does what you put here explain what sexuality looks like to you (i.e., when you imagine it in your mind, do these ideas and concepts come up also?)? If so, how would you define sexuality based on these ideas? If not, how would you change your definition? B. Blackness • Do you think that being Black affects the way you think about or experience sex? If so, how? Bonus Question: what, in your opinion, does sex look like in an ideal Black society?
Part Four: CLOSING	I really appreciate the time you took to have this interview with me. Is there anything that I have not yet asked you that you would like to share about this topic or conversation?

INDEX

Note: Page numbers in *italics* indicate a figure on the corresponding page. Page numbers followed by 'n' indicate a note.

acts of service 67
aesthetics 57–59
African Americans: and anti-Blackness 11; facing disparities 3; insecurity among LGBTQ+ individuals 3; racialized sexualization on 13; sexual ideation of 2, 8, 12; sexuality among 4, 22, 115; social expression 42; usefulness of grounded theory to sexological research on 158
Afrocentric Decolonizing Queer Theory (ADQT) 10
American Social Hygiene Association 114
anti-Blackness 8–11, 18–19n5, 31, 118, 131, 134–135
attraction 46–47

Be-ers, vs. Doers 76
"Black Funk" 10–12
Blackness: anti- 8–11, 18–19n5, 31, 118, 131, 134–135; performative 42–45, 116, 134; and race 129–130; as sexiness 52n1; and sexuality 111–112
Black Sexual Epistemology (BSE) 13–14, 22, 32, 55, 118; in context 110–135; eight channels of sexiness 28–29, *28*; employment of 123–124; model summary 107–108; research study methodology 157–170; as sexological theory 121–122; themes of sexiness in 122–123; as theory of embodiment 117

INDEX

Black sexuality 6, 11, 117–120, 158
Black Skin, White Masks (Fanon) 10
Black studies 111, 121–122
body aesthetics 58
"Box, the" 92–93

Canda, E. 22
Charmaz, K. 158
Chatterjee, P. 22
chemistry, and connection 65
chronic pain 98–99
cognition 55
coital activities 24, 38, 66, 118
colorism 94
commercialism 96–97
communication 69
compassion 38, 67
competence 38–39
comportment 36–40
confidence 37
connection 64–66
Connell, C. 126
'conventionally attractive' people 45, 52n2
corporeality 40–42
Critical Black Studies (CBS) 112
cuddle dates 56, 66
Cunningham, E. C. 11–12, 117

depth 48–49
Diamond, M. 113
disability 98–99
Doers, vs. Be-ers 75–76
double consciousness 10
DuBois, W. E. B. 10

Elliott, S. 126
Ellison, R. 9

emic positionality/epistemological relationship 132–133
emotions/emotional 55; risk-taking 65; vulnerability 65–66, 71
erotic beings 26–28
erotic energy 45–51, 65
erotic self/selves 13, 23, 26–28, 30, 32, 73–88, 90–91, 116; Doer/Be-er 75–76; Journeyer 77–78; Magnet 80–83; Product 83–85; Relator 79–80; sexual brand 75, 85–88
erotophobia 10
ethnosexuality 5, 6
Exploring Black Sexuality (2006) 110
external influences 14, 30, 89–108, 134–135; chronic pain, illness and disability 98–99; commercialism 96–97; hyper-experience of 91; professional identity 105–107; racial maligning 91–96; sexual precocity 101–103; sexual trauma 99–101; technology 103–104
exuded being 25, 27, 28–29, 32, 34–52; comportment 36–40; corporeality 40–42; erotic energy 45–51; performative Blackness 42–45

Fanon, F. 10
fantasy 63–64
fluidity 47–48
Foucault, M. 6–8
"From Theory to Practice: Abolishing Anti-Blackness From the Sex Education Classroom" 144–152

Glaser, B. 158
Goldfarb, E. 124
grounded theory xii, 157–158

Hardy, K. 126
healing 2
"helping professions" 127–128
human sexuality 122–123

identity: professional 105–107; sexual 85
illness/disability 98–99
inanimate objects 41, 83
intelligence 62–63
internet technology 103–104
Invisible Man (Ellison) 9

JanMohamed, A. 7, 8
Johnson, E. P. 42, 119, 122
Johnson, V. 113
Journeyer 77–78

Kinsey, A. 113

Laszloffy, T. A. 126
Lewis, L. 114, 115
Lorde, A. 11
lust 5, 58

Magnet 80–83, 84–85
Malinowski, B. 113
Masters, W. 113
material sex 117
mental excitation 61–64
mind, and emotions 55
miscegenation 8
Morrison, T. 12

multicultural perspective (MCP), in therapeutic practice 126–127
music 60

Nagel, J. 4–5
New World 7
noncoital activities 56, 102

performative Blackness 42–45, 116, 134
personas, erotic 75–88
physiology, and emotion 55
positive affect 70–72
power 7–8, 49–50
pressure 83–84
Product 83–85
professional identity 105–107
public health 114, 115

"quare" theory 119

race/racism 30–32, 31, 116, 120, 122, 127; -based epistemologies 133; and Blackness 129–130; and economics 96; and sexuality 2, 3–4, 111; social construction of 2, 3
Race, Ethnicity, and Sexuality: Intimate Intersections, Forbidden Frontiers (Nagel) 4
racial ideologies 5
racialization xii, 13, 44–45, 116, 127, 134
racialized sexuality, theories of 4–13
racial maligning 91–96
Rajack-Talley, T. A. 133
reciprocity 68–69
relationships 64–70
Relator 79–80
religion 93–94

repressive hypothesis 7
resistance 95
resultant theory 14, 170
Robbins, S. 22

Schroeder, E. 125, 126
self-sovereignty 39
sensory experience 25, 27–29, 32, 53–72; mental excitation 61–64; positive affect 70–72; relationship 64–70; sensual pleasure 56–61, 118
sensual pleasure 56–61, 118
sex: education 113–114, 124–126; material 117; negativity 13, 122, 123; positivity 92, 122, 129; and race 2, 42, 122
sexiness: assessment of 115; categories of 28; as commodity 96; development 12, 13–14, 22–23, 28, 30, 90, 124; eight channels of 28–29, 28; external influences 30; optimal 76; production of 32; sexual health and 133–134; sexuality and 23–26, 27, 128
sexology 113
sexual brand 75, 85–88
Sexual Dimension: A Guide for the Mental Health Practitioner, The (Strean) 128
sexual fulfillment 117
sexual healing 10
sexual health 133–134
sexual ideation 2, 8, 12, 87, 103
sexual identity 85

sexual intercourse 117
sexuality: blackness and 111–112; bourgeoisie 7; concept of 6; counseling and therapy 126–127; education 113, 125, 152; human 122–123; practitionership 114–115, 124; professional 86–87; race and 2, 3–4, 111; in re-membering 12; as "sexiness engineering" 21–33; social construction and function 6; understanding 3–4
sexual morality 5
sexual orientations 85
sexual precocity 101–103
sexual trauma 99–101
Sharma, A. 114
sight, and touch 59
Smedley, A. 3
Smedley, B. 3
smell, and sound 59–60
social discourses 123–124
social norms 6, 77, 94
social work 127–128
sound, smell and 59–60
Stanton, D. C. 7, 8
Staples, R. 110, 111
Stoler, A. 7
Strauss, A. 158
Strean, H. 128
swagger 43
symbolic interaction 22

taste 60–61
technology 103–104
Thomas, G. 2

Thompson, R. F. 52n1
touch, sight and 59
transphobia 82

"unknowable, the" 50

Vargas, J. C. 17n7
vulnerability 65, 102

Whipple, B. 113
wholism theory 11, 12
Williams, H. 10

Yancy, G. 8–10